DEATH OF

DEATH
of a
Princess
Making sense of a nation's grief

John Drane

David Hilborn

Heather Wraight

Evelyn Sharpe

Tony Walter

Chris Sugden (Editor)

SILVER FISH PUBLISHING
LONDON

First published in Great Britain 1998 by
Silver Fish Publishing.

British Library Cataloguing in Publication Data
A record for this book is available from the British Library

ISBN 1 902134 05 2

Printed and bound in Great Britain by
Cox & Wyman, Reading, Berks

Silver Fish Publishing is a division of
Silver Fish Creative Marketing Ltd
44c Fermoy Road, Maida Vale
London W9 3NH

CONTENTS

ACKNOWLEDGEMENTS

Our warm thanks to the English Lausanne Movement, Jeremy Mudditt Publishing Services, and Anthea Cousins for their role in making this publication possible.

CONTRIBUTORS

Rev Dr John Drane is lecturer in practical theology at Aberdeen University and author of *Faith in a Changing Culture* (London, HarperCollins, 1997)

Rev Dr David Hilborn is minister of the City Temple, Holborn Viaduct, secretary of the Evangelical Alliance ACUTE (The Alliance's Commission on Unity and Truth among Evangelicals) and author of *Picking up the Pieces – Can Evangelicals Adapt to Contemporary Culture* (Hodder, 1997).

Heather Wraight works for Christian Research and is co-editor of the *UK Christian Handbook* (London, Christian Research, 1997)

Dr Evelyn Sharpe is a consultant psychiatrist in the National Health Service and a member of Interhealth.

Dr Tony Walter is lecturer in Sociology at the University of Reading, and course director of MA in Death and Society. He is author of *A Long Way from Home* (Exeter, Paternoster, 1979), *The Revival of Death* (London, Routledge, 1994), and *The Eclipse of Eternity: a sociology of the afterlife* (Basingstoke, Macmillan, 1996).

FOREWORD

The emotional reaction displayed after the death of the Princess of Wales was an unprecedented phenomenon. It was described as the greatest spiritual experience the country had experienced this century. The flowers, the media coverage, thousands of people openly weeping were new to us. This book suggests some answers to the question of why this happened.

As Director of the Leprosy Mission, one of Diana's six remaining charities, and the only one with a Christian foundation, I spent time talking to her on long flights abroad, waiting for events to start, and at her home in Kensington Palace. Having every material asset a person could wish, Diana was a seeker after wider spiritual truth and many of the conversations we had centred around orthodox Christian belief. The media, however, especially sections of the press, seemed interested only in her visits to mediums and astrologers.

My father was involved in politics and as a young man I met three Prime Ministers and a President of the United States. I was aware of the power which came from their office. The Princess's power, and there is no doubt that she was very powerful, came from her extraordinary compassion, which to those who witnessed it was entirely genuine. On one occasion we visited a refugee camp near the border between Zimbabwe and Mozambique. There were some leprosy patients among the thousands of refugees. The Princess made a point of stooping and touching every one of them. As our small group was leaving, out of the sight of the press, the Princess said something too quietly for me to hear, and ran off to our left. Within a few seconds she was sitting on the ground with a leprosy patient, who was too weak to join the others, her fine hands holding the stump of an arm where once another hand had been. One woman in pain speaking to another woman, also in pain.

People recognised this compassion intuitively and this was reflected in the outpouring of emotion. The candles, the flowers, the silence of London in the two weeks after her death were motivated by a hungering after answers, a folk religion. Numbers attending the funeral, including those who watched on television, were greater than anyone had expected, and they were genuinely taking part. People lining the route, and in the parks in London, and at home, followed the words of the service and joined in the Lord's Prayer. For the church this was an opportunity to minister and find new ways of explaining the truths of the gospel.

There are signs that people want the Princess's work to continue, and that the causes she supported, including The Leprosy Mission, now have a higher profile than before.

This book helps to explore what happened in September 1997. If people are inspired to be more compassionate in their private and public lives, then the life and death of Diana, Princess of Wales will be of eternal significance.

Part of the royalties will be donated to The Leprosy Mission, Goldhay Way, Orton Goldhay, Peterborough PE2 5GZ, whose patron was Diana, Princess of Wales from 1990 until her death in 1997.

Dr Tony Lloyd
Executive Director,
The Leprosy Mission

INTRODUCTION

History books will record that within a thousand days of the end of the twentieth century, tens of thousands of subjects of the Queen of Great Britain stood in Hyde Park and prayed in public, following the lead of the Archbishop of Canterbury, at the funeral of a royal princess. Why? Was this a totally new phenomenon of mourning fuelled by the mass media and informed by do-it-yourself spirituality? Or did it represent a return to powerful and vital forces in the life of the human community, and does it offer a challenge to the church to renounce its obsession with rationalism and modernity and return to its own roots?

A clash of cultures

'A landmark day' is how Will Hutton, author of *The State We're In* and editor of *The Observer*, described the day of Princess Diana's funeral. It was a landmark day in terms of its constitutional implications for monarchy in that it asserted the will of the people as citizens rather than as subjects. It was also a landmark day as the people interpreted Diana's death in terms of national identity, what they were proud of and what spoke for them. The Diana story has run and run because it makes its appeal at every level: love, family, personal tragedy, intrigue, politics, power and religion. Her funeral was the occasion when the public face of post-modern religion and spirituality clashed with an older culture. The struggle between the two cultures continues in conversation, newspaper columns, books and articles as people seek to interpret not only what happened but themselves.

Like others, I had not expected to be so moved by Princess Diana's death. I left Britain on Sunday August 31st as Diana's body came back from France and I arrived back at 9 a.m. on the following Saturday to see on TV the coffin leave from Kensington Palace. But during 'I Vow to Thee My Country', I welled up at the words 'The dearest and the best'. For with others, I felt proud of Diana. For all her 'complexity' as it is called, she had represented virtues of which we could be justly proud.

She gave love, and sought it. She knew people need love, and without embarrassment sought out those who acknowledged their need. When she and her husband appeared on the balcony of Buckingham Palace after their wedding, the crowds called out for them to kiss. No one had been seen to kiss in public on that balcony before. The picture of their kiss went around the world. And the world began to fall in love with Diana from that point. She responded to the people. She broke with convention. She was not embarrassed to show her love. For many she was like the child in the story of the Emperor's new clothes. She pointed out that some ways of doing things were, in her words, 'hopeless'. Her unembarrassed compassion tended to show up what was false and fake. Just as she had not been too embarrassed to kiss her husband on the palace balcony, so she shook hands with AIDS sufferers, and spoke up for the victims of land mines, which others regarded as a military necessity.

But others have accused Princess Diana and those who mourned her deeply of themselves being the fakes. They felt uneasy then and continue to feel uneasy now about the outpouring of grief. This again expresses the clash of cultures. Such people feel far more comfortable with the ordered control that stood our parents in good stead through two world wars. But that society had many other personal and social supports through which people could find human warmth.

In today's more individualist society, the new culture seeks space for the compassionate, the emotional, the feminine, the spontaneous, and for the excluded and the socially disreputable. This new culture found expression in the funeral. The shared experience of the funeral procession gave a sense of unity and connectedness. Instead of fanfares, troops of soldiers, and dignitaries, there was the contradiction of a campaigner against landmines being carried on a gun carriage followed by representatives of charities.

But contradiction is itself part of the new culture. It focuses on caring for the immediate human need here and now, not waiting for the ideal grand solution. It objects to landmines because they hurt the innocent, whatever the arguments about military strategy.

The new culture embarrasses the older one, especially if the older holds power. So the old culture recoils from the expressions of the new culture. Public expressions of grief and loss are condemned as mawkish sentimentality.

In witnessing to the love of Jesus, those who are Christians should not find themselves wedded to either culture. But we should not pretend that we can witness to Jesus' love apart from these cultures. We should start from where people are, not from where they should be.

Tony Blair cleared his diary. Sports fixtures were postponed, and shops were closed for half a day. Saturday saw a huge open-air church service. People stood and sang, and said the Lord's Prayer. Some churches like St Philip's Church in Cambridge rented a huge video-screen, and invited people to watch the funeral along with others in church. Others held services of remembrance to minister to what people were feeling. There was a desire for contact, to play a part, to be there. There was a yearning for something beyond, a feeling of wanting to have some way of expressing together shock, loss, grief and how to address the void together.

So we witnessed the funeral of a charismatic leader. But the Old Testament record of judges, kings and prophets suggests that humanity does not require just charisma, spontaneity, and empathy; it also needs covenant – law, loyalty, faithfulness. People have been calling for stricter laws, especially against the invasion of privacy. But legalism is no answer. France has laws against speeding and drunk driving. These were not enough to prevent the dreadful accident. People need new hearts not just a Queen of Hearts.

How does what people have been feeling and expressing about the humanity which Diana represented relate to Jesus? There are many resonances between the story of Diana and people's response to her, and the story of Jesus. This is entirely to be expected because the truly human finds its fulfilment in Jesus.

What Bible text would suit a sermon on the passing of Diana? While Elton John sang so movingly of 'A Candle in the Wind', Christians can point to the Light of the World, the source of all such candles which cannot be put out. An archdeacon from Nigeria thought of the words to Jesus on the Emmaus Road: 'We had thought he was the one to redeem Israel' (Luke 24:21). Many had thought, as she had hoped, that she could humanize some of Britain's institutions starting with a future monarch. Paul's affirmation that 'the greatest is love' (1 Corinthians 13:13) which was read at the memorial service, roots the concern and search for love at the heart of the universe. Jesus of course touched lepers and mixed with the socially disreputable. His humanitarian work was suspected by the powerful, but was welcomed by those 'who knew they were sick' (Matthew 9:12). People's desire that something good must come from this tragedy can be founded on 'All things work for good' (Romans 8:28), and in the conviction that 'Except a grain of wheat fall into the ground and die, it abides alone' (John 12:21).

I have not heard anyone ask 'Why did God allow this?' But people are prepared to reflect on the nature of their own response which has taken them by surprise. We must witness to the gospel in relation to people's yearnings. Otherwise this upsurge of religious expression and searching which leads some people to intend to change their lives, will end in disappointment, cynicism and rejection. It was very telling to see how, after the memorial service the crowds wandered down the Mall at the end of a week of grief, 'as sheep without a shepherd' – now that the focus of their grief was gone.

John Bird and John Fortune in a satirical sketch on Rory Bremner's show on Channel 4 television at the end of 1997 appeared as two middle-aged men talking in a pub 'snug'. One spoke of how he had been so moved by the events of Diana's death and funeral that his life had been changed. His drinking partner sank deeper into depression because he realized he could not change his life as he had been out of the country at the time. The sketch pierced the exclusivity and shallowness of the change to which some people laid claim. The Christian claim by contrast is that such change is always possible through a relationship with Jesus Christ who is always accessible.

This religious expression will continue to develop. The 'people's wreath' assembled itself on the funeral hearse as it threaded through the crowds. The middle classes in the last few years have rejected flowers in favour of charity donations at funerals. But footballers and other folk heroes are regularly commemorated with flowers at impromptu shrines. So the people's simple bouquets combined with contributions to Diana's charities show a warmer way of responding. The next stage will be pilgrimage to the shrine of 'the lady of the lake' when Earl Spencer opens Althorp's flower-bedecked gates again.

Christians must be ready. New Testament faith, as John Goldingay points out, has no holy places or shrines. And as David Macpherson the vicar of Great Brington pointed out – 'She is not here, she is with the Lord'. The Archbishop of Canterbury spoke of her real faith in God. Thora Hird told how her favourite hymn was 'Breathe on Me Breath of God'. Where could someone with her history of loveless rejection find the love she expressed? She had received little of the usual nurture in life. Her mother and father divorced when she was six. She tried to win her husband's love, and all along he also loved another. She was divorced, we are told, against her will. She responded not by denying the need for love, but by speaking openly that everyone needs to know they are loved, everyone needs a hug.

Diana and the people's response has been suspect to some because for them it does not represent the right way to relate to God. Unlike Mother Teresa, she was no nun. But her love for the socially embarrassing brings to mind Jesus' commendation of the rich tax-collector who stood at a distance in prayer. He knew he was rejected by the Pharisee who was in the temple praying at the same time. The Pharisee established his social standing in prayer, gave his credentials of his good works, and prayed with himself. The tax-collector knew his vulnerability. He knew he was rejected by God as he would not even look up to heaven. He cried out for mercy, in his sins (Luke 18:9-14).

This was a real clash of cultures in Jesus story. And we have a clash of cultures in the response to Diana. On the one hand the children and the young, those old enough to be her parents, the poor and the disabled, as well as socially unacceptable people of wealth and fame, all loved her. On the other, some, particularly people in socially powerful positions, called her a paranoid and manipulative woman. They could not ignore her, for not only was she at the top of their tree, but loved to obsession by many of those at the bottom. If the socially powerful rejected her, they risked the displeasure of the people and the media. The very stone which the old builders of our social fabric rejected, looks set to become the cornerstone for the future development of our national life. In this very real clash, Christian witness is not to any one cultural expression of the Christian faith, but to ensuring that in all cultures, and through cultural shifts, we interpret the gospel in a way in which people can hear and to which they can respond.

It will be a long time before we fully fathom why Diana, who did only what so many charity and voluntary workers do around the world, was any different in her impact. It may well be that more information will come to light in coming months and years about her private life, her relationships with the media, and about who was allowed to say what in the media presentation of her death and memorial service, which is at the moment the privileged information of those who are not divulging it. Such information may lead to a revision of some perspectives but is beside the point of this book. The public response to Diana's death is a fact of history, whether or not that response was manipulated by the withholding of information. It gives a clear if surprising indication of the nature of the British soil into which the seed of the Christian gospel is to be sown in the twenty-first century. We need to reflect on the significance of people's grief for the people's princess and how the people of God may minister to it.

To this end 150 people gathered at City Temple, Holborn Viaduct, London, on Saturday February 7th 1998 to spend a day sponsored by the English Lausanne Movement, reflecting on the significance of the national and global reaction to the Death of Diana, Princess of Wales. They were resourced by the Minister of the City Temple, Rev Dr David Hilborn; Dr Tony Walter, lecturer in sociology at the University of Reading; Rev Dr John Drane, director of the Centre for the Study of Christianity and Society at the University of Stirling; Rev Dr Tony Lloyd, the director of the Leprosy Mission, one of the six final charities of which Diana was patron; Heather Wraight, a broadcaster and researcher with Christian Research; and Dr Evelyn Sharpe, psychiatrist, with Interhealth. Peter Lace, a minister in the house church movement, spoke of the 'Diana prophecy', which referred to flowers being placed in all Britain's cities. The focus of the day was on the immense national and global outpouring of grief.

Following the presentations and discussions, it was suggested that the material on the main theme should be available to a wider audience. Hence this book is offered as a Christian comment on the event of Diana's death and the mourning that followed it, not to bring praise or blame on either the central figure or the cast of millions, but to prompt understanding of this human phenomenon that took us all by surprise, so that we may better understand ourselves.

Society lives

Dr Evelyn Sharpe recalls the sights, sounds and feelings of that first week in September 1997. She parallels the national experience of grief with the personal grieving cycle. She suggests that grief without hope leads to despair, and that true hope is a trust in what we believe, not merely a feeling. Heather Wraight, herself a broadcaster, examines the role of the media in pursuing Diana when alive and discusses the codes of practice that may prevent a repetition of those events.

Dr Tony Walter stresses that mourning rituals are the most fundamental way in which people band together against death. In traditional societies where people are known to each other, the death of a village member affects everyone whether they know them well or not. In the process of urbanization and modernization only close friends and relatives know of one's bereavement. So most of us live most of the time oblivious of others' griefs. But when a soldier or a schoolchild dies, the whole regiment or the whole school are drawn in and the village situation is recreated. In the death of Diana, the whole of society knew. There was reversion to mourning on a global scale into which everyone got drawn whether they liked it or not. Private individuals were dragged into public grief, and those who objected failed to see the obligations of membership of a global community.

Diana had such a powerful impact because she symbolized precisely those caring and feminine values which those at the top of the individualistic rationalistic society of the west in the eighties said did not count. She indicated that there was more to life than making money. So the national coming together in grief and mourning was a symbolic reconstruction of the very society which Margaret Thatcher had declared did not exist. Diana communicated in non-cognitive ways. Her touching of lepers and AIDS victims was well-known. Tony Lloyd pointed out that Mother Teresa told Diana to touch the suffering; and Mother Teresa said that her inspiration for this was Jesus.

John Drane notes that Diana had often been perceived in redemptive terms. 'Candle in the Wind' spoke of her as 'the grace that placed itself where lives were torn apart'. She worked as a kindergarten nanny and her true significance was noticed only when it was too late; she was concerned with the poor; she brought a real touch of joy and love into the lives of those she met; she was hunted down by authority figures; she is seen as more than human; there were pilgrimages to see her and shrines to her memory.

All this indicates a popular desire for a large story to make sense of the whole of life. People want 'myths' to explain what is going on. They are fed up with the reductionism that characterises the way humans relate in society in modernity. They want a large 'metanarrative'. So while people do not like 'modernity and soulless rationality', and are therefore 'post-modern' with a hyphen, they are not totally isolated individuals making up their own identities as they go along. They are not therefore 'postmodern' without a hyphen in the way that the prophets of postmodernity would like them to be, isolated individuals creating their own different identities in exercise of their unfettered choice.

John Drane and Tony Walter urge that churches should not seek to construct programmes to reach a new kind of unbeliever. Rather those in the churches should begin to understand themselves and how to relate to the response shown to Diana's death. The form that much Christianity takes is rationalistic and institutional. But people are not seeking rational explanations. Evelyn Sharpe argues that the spirituality she saw among mourners at Kensington Palace was neither Christian nor gave evidence that people were expecting the Church to supply answers for their yearning. People do want the faith that gets you through the night, through suffering and tragedy. The standard answers of the orthodox appear simplistic and irrelevant. People are searching for spirituality and community.

The question this raises is 'Are the churches spiritual?' In the culture of reductionist modernity the churches focus on justice and social issues. They are full of people doing good things. This is right, but not sufficient. Many churches have bought into a rationalist culture and seem to have blanked out the sense of the numinous and spiritual. But people are fed up with an exclusively cognitive culture. As commitment to other modern institutions declines in society, churches which are modernist will also feel the draught. Churches need to recover the numinous. Could our theologians articulate a theology of angels? In the incarnation the word of God became tactile, symbolic, and intuitive. We have often put the word become flesh back into words again.

John Drane related at the conference how on the evening of Diana's death, while speaking at Shetland Bible Week, his wife Olive, who has been engaged in an internationally acclaimed ministry of Christian clowning since the death of one of their own children some years ago, put on her own clown's clothes and spoke of the spirituality that is born out of tragedy. As she applied white grease paint to her face she spoke of the new start offered by God as we open ourselves to the possibility of a new creation won by Christ; the colours spoke of the life and vibrancy of the Holy Spirit. She ended by putting crosses on her eyes, showing that we need to see the world as God sees it, through the cross. John and Olive then asked for those who wanted to see the world as God sees it to come for crosses to be marked on their eyes, or hands, or feet. Immediately most of those present responded to the invitation to have a tactile and visible symbol to relate to, and went out into the night, marked by the sign of the cross. One woman was asked by her husband at home what this meant. She said she wanted to see him as God saw him, and love and appreciate him. The next day her husband joined her at a Christian event for the first time in his life, longing to have the same healing encounter that his wife had experienced. Throughout the week, many people sought out the Dranes, attracted by the prospect of themselves receiving the mark of the cross, and the possibilities of new life which it symbolised.

Tony Walter urged that members of churches become more aware of how to support and minister to people who are bereaved and grieving. Anniversary and memorial services for those who have died perform an important ministry to those who still carry their loss.

What of Diana's own spirituality? Was she, as David Hilborn suggests, an archetype of the postmodern pick and mix, do it yourself spirituality, seeking salvation from a wide and conflicting range of options? Tony Lloyd referred to her genuine desire to seek, her belief in the power of prayer, her compassion to the marginalized and her remarkable insight into the probable background of the penitent thief on the cross and the promise of the Lord that he would be in paradise. His conclusion was that if we can only seek God with his help, then her seeking was evidence of God's work in her life, and with Cardinal Hume he knew God would deal with her mercifully as with us all.

John Drane pointed out that, according to Acts 17, Paul did not rubbish the spirituality he saw in Athens. He rather pointed to the altar of the unknown God, to what they knew, and declared to them Jesus. How may we find the altars of the unknown God in our society, and meet the need for the spiritual reality they express? Perhaps the millions of flowers laid in our cities last September were placed on that altar. To meet this need, we do not need to reinvent the church but to return to our roots in the incarnation.

Jesus lives! Diana lives?

In the incarnation, we meet the love of God in Jesus. Diana was crying out for the love she never received. The ordinary people of the world tried to show that they loved her and wanted her to find love. Jesus says he gives this unconditional love, love for the loveless, love that is transparent, love that does not cling to its own position, love that embarrasses those in power. He was put to death because his love was embarrassing. But he rose again and lives. Those who die in the faith of Jesus will one day live again. In a way that might recall Jesus she did not cling on to her own position but associated with the lowly. Like children she was not embarrassed by showing love, and Jesus said that unless we become like children we cannot enter his kingdom. From the testimony of the Archbishop of Canterbury, Tony Lloyd and Thora Hird, I honestly hope that we can say that Diana lives; that she has gone to that great children's home in the sky which is the source of all love; where she will have plenty of children to love; where she will find the forgiveness that she and we all need, and get the biggest hug of all from the God and Father of all; and where her unembarrassed love will embarrass no one.

Rev Dr Chris Sugden
Director of academic affairs
Oxford Centre for Mission Studies

DIANA'S DEATH

Public and private grief

Evelyn Sharpe

It is the ritual not the fact
That brings a held emotion to
its breaking point. This man I knew
Only a little, by his death
Shows me a love I thought I lacked
And all the stirrings underneath

It is the calm, the solemn thing,
Not the distracted mourner's cry
Or the cold place where dead things lie,
That teaches me I cannot claim
To stand aside. These tears which sting –
Are they from sorrow or from shame?

Elizabeth Jennings

When people said they remembered exactly where they were when they heard about the assassination of John F. Kennedy I felt something of a failure for not having registered so important an event. Being only ten, having no TV at home and having little concept of who JFK was or what he signified meant that his death had no impact on my life at all. I do remember three years later being told my father had died, and I remember in 1987, as I was driving along a Belfast street, hearing on the radio that a bomb had gone off at the War Memorial in my home-town, and I shall probably always remember waking on a Sunday morning in August 1997 to hear that Diana, Princess of Wales, had been killed in a car accident in Paris.

Diana

I never met Diana, did not love her, disapproved of certain things she said and did and was sometimes irritated by the constant media coverage of her activities both public and private. As a psychiatrist I occasionally wondered what I would say if she turned up in my office and what her various therapists had done for her. As a woman I sometimes envied her good looks and her style. I admired her involvement with marginalized groups, those with leprosy especially, her willingness to touch and embrace, and her ability to empathize with and relate to everyone she met. I speculated on how her own experiences influenced her interactions with people and her choice of good causes. I joined in church prayers for her as a member of the royal family and sometimes prayed for her personally. Thus, like millions of others, I have my story of what Diana meant to me. She was, in a small or big way, part of the lives of very many people throughout the world and because her life had personal significance to them they grieved at her death.

'A family in grief, in a country of mourning, before a world in shock' was how Earl Spencer described it. The country's mourning was very public yet it was not merely an expression of a sense of national loss or sympathy for a family bereaved. In Diana's life many people saw a reflection of their own and her death was a personal tragedy. She came from a broken home, knew what it was like to be pulled between unhappy parents, and did not achieve very much at school. Then, when all that seemed to be unimportant because she had married a man she loved and had two sons, she experienced separation and divorce, preceded by, on her own account, years of deep unhappiness, betrayal and rejection. She developed an eating disorder, tried to harm herself, and became depressed. All these are not uncommon experiences nowadays. This was reflected by some of the messages in the books of condolence. 'I have a daughter who went through depression' wrote one, and, 'I can relate to her because I've just gone through a marriage break-up' wrote another.

Diana's brother described her as 'a very insecure person at heart, almost childlike in her desire to do good for others so she could release herself from deep feelings of unworthiness of which her eating disorders were merely a symptom'. Disorders of the self, difficulties in establishing personal identity, struggles with feelings of low self-worth and low self-esteem are common to our society. People could see in Diana many of their own feelings and struggles.

People could also identify with Diana's various strategies for trying to deal with her difficulties. These strategies were in keeping with the 'try it and if it works, fine' approach of modern culture.

She talked to all kinds of counsellors and therapists, tried alternative therapies, and pursued physical fitness. The inconsistencies and contradictions between the different approaches did not seem to matter. At the time of her death there was a perception that she was, finally, secure in herself, confident in her role and happy. Taken at 'her most beautiful and radiant and when she had joy in her private life' was how Earl Spencer described it. Whether or not that was a true perception, or another illusion that would have been shattered in time we do not know. But her death seemed even more tragic than if it had come at a less happy time.

Diana embodied a kind of ideal for many. She did worthwhile work and combined it with being a loving mother who not only had fun with her boys but showed them how to care for others. She also enjoyed herself with friends, partied and had exotic holidays. She mixed with outcasts, marginalized and neglected people, showing compassion and affection. She remained attractive and well-groomed whatever she did, and though she mixed with famous and influential people she could also drop into a neighbouring café for coffee or take a walk in a public park with friends. She was not an ideal of unreachable perfection. She was seen as somehow attainable, reachable, 'one of us', and so gained a place in people's hearts. She could also be manipulative, foolish, even malicious. So she aroused ambivalent responses which made the grieving for her death more complicated and confusing since grieving is more straightforward when the relationship with the deceased has been good.

Grief, guilt and anger

Diana's death also brought a sense of guilt, a reaction which is commonly part of grief. Guilt is often mixed with anger, another common reaction which was very evident after Diana's death, and was expressed against the media and against the royal family, in an almost wild way at times. Hostility was shown towards those who were not joining in the mourning or were seen as not mourning in an acceptable way. Earl Spencer echoed the anger in his funeral address and voiced some anger against God who, 'granted her but half a life', adding 'we will all feel cheated always that you were taken from us so young'.

People also grieved because a dream had died. We mourn the loss of what might have been just as we mourn the loss of what was. The fairy story of the wedding had turned out to be a much darker tale but people still hoped. There was hope that she might be happy, that her sons might have an untroubled existence after the traumas of the divorce, even that there might be a reconciliation; all these were dashed. Many of the cards and messages after her death showed a longing to keep the dream intact. 'Dodi and Diana together in heaven, happy forever', and 'Diana free from suffering and persecution' were common themes.

Among the crowds mourning Diana were those who were expressing grief at other losses, some from a long time ago, reawakened by the princess's death. People who felt their grieving had had to be suppressed or cut short found permission to grieve openly, to express their own sorrows in a society usually ill at ease with death and grief.

In the public reaction were all the normal elements of grief – numbness, disbelief, sadness, questioning and guilt. Many words were spoken and written as people tried to express their feelings. But, especially at first, there was the wordless sorrow expressed in gatherings and symbols. In the Old Testament story of Job, his friends found the sadness to be so great that they could only sit in silence for days. For some it was important to be in a place associated with Diana. So the crowds flowed to Kensington Palace and elsewhere.

The rituals of mourning

The rituals of the mourning provided a way for emotion to be expressed and gave comfort. They also supplied a structure which meant that while the grieving was not out of control, it was not suppressed. Laying flowers and gifts, lighting candles, keeping vigil at the palaces and along the funeral route, writing in books of condolence, coming together to watch the funeral on big screens, and attending church services were all ways of acknowledging personal loss and also of identifying with public grief. 'I had to see the coffin to actually believe she is gone', said a woman at the funeral.

The rituals that gave such comfort and release for emotion were not primarily Christian. I walked around Kensington Palace the night before the funeral. Little groups of people were sitting on the grass in silent circles, heads bowed, around clusters of burning candles, like worshippers at a shrine yet which was not Christian. Tree trunks were covered in flowers and messages, resembling pagan use of sacred trees. The messages implored and anticipated Diana's help from heaven. There was spirituality, spiritual longing, the sense of the transcendent which death brings, but little evidence that people expected the church to supply any answers to the yearnings.

Christian truths were spoken and sung at the funeral service. But Elton John's song 'Goodbye England's Rose' was what most people wanted to hear and Earl Spencer's address evoked the applause. His courageous and bold speech echoed many of the thoughts and feelings of the people listening and people wanted to acknowledge that. He did make reference to God but not with any obvious expectation of help from him or hope in him.

Moving on

Once the funeral was over and the flowers and tributes cleared away life for most returned to normal as it does after any tragedy. It was helpful to some to have the official ending of flower-laying pronounced, giving permission to move on. Moving on has been difficult as individuals and groups have been trying to decide on suitable memorials. Perhaps the uncertainty over what to do reflects the difficulty people have in thinking about Diana's death, not in remembering it or recalling the emotion, but in putting it into a coherent mental framework.

Release of emotion may be cathartic. But the relief may not last and may bring no lasting change. Ways of thinking influence feelings as shown by the effectiveness of cognitive therapy in depression, and the right cognitive framework is needed if feelings are not to govern us completely. Grief without hope leads to despair and true hope is a trust in what we believe, not merely a feeling.

> *In you, our dead enigma, all the strains*
> *Criss-cross in useless equilibrium*

Seamus Heaney wrote those words in a poem in memory of an Irish Catholic soldier killed in France in 1917. If there is no answer for the anger and frustration death brings then a 'useless equilibrium' may be the most we can expect.

People may seek substitutes for Diana and bring pressure on her sons to be her replacement. For them the grieving continues and their sense of loss may grow as time goes on. Tensions buried in the initial overwhelming grief may resurface. The cynicism over good intentions which was largely suspended has already shown signs of reappearing. In his book written after a catastrophic experience of bereavement Gerald L. Sittser says, 'It is not the experience of loss that becomes the defining moment of our lives, for that is as inevitable as death, which is the last loss awaiting us all. It is how we respond to loss that matters. That response will largely determine the quality, the direction, and the impact of our lives.'

I remember being told that suffering could make one bitter or better but I have learnt that it can also leave us unaffected. It remains to be seen whether the grief, both personal and public, over the death of Diana will result in any lasting change.

THE DEATH OF A PRINCESS

Lessons for the churches

John Drane

From the moment she married into the British royal family Diana, Princess of Wales, was always in the public spotlight. At first, she was merely admired as one of the rich and beautiful people, but then as the fairytale dream evaporated and the drama of her real-life struggles, both with herself and her family relationships, unfolded in the public arena, she was embraced into the hearts not only of her own nation, but by people throughout the world who identified with her struggle to find meaning and fulfilment in life. The ups and downs of her life became a powerful reflection of the experience of many others at the end of the twentieth century: full of potential, eager to do good, infused with genuine compassion, but beaten by the system and left wounded by the wayside, wondering if and how the pieces might ever be put together again. By the time she died in the early hours of Sunday August 31st 1997, the suffering she had endured, her newly-found personal happiness with Dodi al-Fayedh, and her much-vaunted determination to stand alongside the disadvantaged and the marginalized seemed to reflect more than just Diana's personal story. Britain was still enjoying the wave of political euphoria that followed the election of a new government only three months previously, and the princess's emergence into new life was an appropriate symbol for the mood of the nation. She had given us a tantalizing glimpse of what the world could be like if we were all kinder and more compassionate, even in the midst of much insecurity. It was inevitable that her death would stir people at the deepest levels of the human psyche. For in a real sense she was a symbol of that combination of brokenness and healing which touches all our lives. Even so, few of us were prepared for the amazing expressions of public anguish that lasted for several weeks after her death, and indeed still continue in many different forms not only in Britain but all over the world.

This was not the first time Britain had seen such outpourings of mass grief, and there are any number of historical precedents to which one can point, both ancient and modern. One can look as far back as the public response to the murder of Archbishop Thomas Becket in Canterbury (1170), while in the nineteenth century the deaths of the Duke of Wellington (1852) and William Gladstone (1898) were both marked by outpourings of public grief, while the death of Queen Victoria in 1901 and the way the end of the First World War (1918) was transformed into an annual national ritual, provide early twentieth century examples of the impact of tragedy on the national consciousness.

It is tempting to regard the responses to Diana's death as merely the most recent example of this historical phenomenon. But there are many aspects of it which are different, and significantly so. For what happened during September 1997 was part of a developing pattern of devotional practice within British culture that can be traced over the last two decades in public responses to (among others) the sinking of the *Herald of Free Enterprise* (1983), the disaster at the Hillsborough football stadium (1989), and the shootings at Dunblane Primary School (1996) – not to mention the spontaneous creation of shrines at the scenes of road accidents on all our major highways. I want to suggest that what took place following Diana's death, far from being an anomalous expression of a maverick spirituality, was actually a pivotal moment in the evolution of a new popular spirituality within western culture.

If that is a correct understanding, it will demand some reappraisal of the secularization thesis embraced uncritically by much contemporary sociology of religion. It will also, however – and this is my main purpose here – present a significant challenge to Christians in relation to the mission of the church in the contemporary world. To expand on this, I propose first to highlight some key aspects of this emerging popular spirituality, before moving on to comment briefly on the wider cultural context in which it is taking place, particularly in relation to the perceived shift from modernity to post-modernity, and the status of conventional religion. Finally, I will offer some comments on what it might mean for Christian mission, and the task of the church as we move towards the new century.

The nature of popular spirituality

There are two fundamental frames of reference within which we can begin to understand what happened following Diana's death. First, and most visibly, when people went into the streets and open spaces to mark their grief, they were engaged in a form of pilgrimage. Watching events as they unfolded on television was, however, a more accessible prospect for some people, and I believe this can best be understood as a form of vigil. Many people of course did both. The central focus of this paper, though, is on the public displays of anguish.

Recent discussion on pilgrimage is characterized on the one hand by those who seek to understand it in the context of the established social structures and, on the other, by those who prefer to see it as a more eclectic phenomenon. Paradoxically, the Diana experience lends support to both these perceptions, while also challenging them both and suggesting that pilgrimage in the post-modern world may be an even more diffuse phenomenon than was previously imagined. Several aspects are particularly noteworthy here.

In their pioneering work, anthropologists Victor and Edith Turner sought to understand pilgrimage by relating it to traditional rites of passage, emphasizing the themes of separation (leaving home), liminality (the journey, visit to the shrine, transforming encounter with the sacred), followed by reincorporation (going home with a new perspective). Those who joined in the mass outpourings of grief following Diana's death clearly had a strong urge to be there, wherever 'there' might be in any particular locality. They were experiencing what Durkheim called 'collective effervescence', and which the Turners identify somewhat differently as the creation of 'communitas' – something that, however it be described, clearly plays a key role in all forms of Christian pilgrimage. But there was one crucial difference. For whereas today's Christian pilgrims tend to move out of the world into the safe spaces of like-minded people, all the recent examples of mass grieving have been more like medieval pilgrimages, with people leaving the safe spaces of family and home, to go into the more dangerous space of the world.

This fact alone raises important missiological questions, for those locations that were regarded as safe spaces where the search for new meaning might occur were not the traditional sacred places of western spirituality (churches). On the whole, they were public spaces that became sacred space, sacralized not by the rituals of religiously authorized persons, but by becoming almost a spatial extension of the interior spirituality of the mass of people who visited them. In central London, parks and other open spaces functioned in this way, while elsewhere it was often shopping malls and council offices. In some ways, this was no surprise, for there was already a strong pilgrimage tradition attached to Diana, and perhaps it was natural for people to grieve in the same places as they would have expected to see her, bearing the same gifts in death as they had done in life.

In that light, the fact that people did not, on the whole, go to churches, need not by itself be so unusual. But there can be no doubt that the preference for the sacralizing of new spaces was in large measure the natural outcome of a growing conviction within our culture generally, that religious institutions have lost sight of the spiritual, and therefore people need to take responsibility for their own religious quest for meaning. It is also significant that people preferred to confront their pain in the most dangerous space of all – the street, the very place where she met her death, and previously had been hunted by the paparazzi – rather than retreating to 'safer' surroundings. Underwriting this was an implied questioning of the value of the prepackaged answers to tragedy that are often given by the representatives of organized religion, and a willingness to engage with the big issues that suggests a greater spiritual maturity in the population at large than conventionally religious people generally allow. In the process, we witnessed the emergence of a self-consciously do-it-yourself pilgrimage style, with little concern for whether people were following recognized cultural rules or formally sanctioned procedures, if only because there were no inherited models for doing this kind of thing. Inevitably, a number of 'unwritten' rules of our culture were broken, but in such a way as to rewrite the nature of the cultural conventions which will now be passed on to future generations. People wept openly in the streets, they threw flowers at Diana's coffin, they prayed in parks and in shopping centres, and they not only exposed their young children to the tragedy, but adopted their insights in seeking for resolution. These and other similar features can only be described as significantly counter-cultural.

In addition to these general characteristics, a number of other features also emerged as having special significance, not only in the aftermath of Diana's death, but also in the context of the 1996 Dunblane shootings – a coincidence which encourages me to propose that what we have seen is more than a merely fortuitous product of unexpected circumstances, and in fact provides evidence of some crucial shifts in the character of popular spirituality, indeed in the nature of our culture.

Spontaneity

A key feature in both episodes was the emergence of a spontaneous, creation-centred spirituality, by which I mean a spirituality rooted in the reality of the human condition as part of the cosmos, rather than in the inherited patterns of the rationality of western culture. Indeed, the dominance of this rationality within our culture was widely regarded as a significant factor in the sequence of cause-and-effect leading to both these tragedies. By contrast, the materials used in the construction of pilgrim shrines were all strongly 'creation-centred', with flowers, flames, and other natural materials, building and elaborating on the locus of the shrines themselves (which were almost entirely outdoors). It is tempting to see here evidence of some tension between the serious search for spiritual meaning that was happening on the streets, and the usual ways in which Christians deal with such matters, if not the actual way in which the church related to these specific tragedies.

Was this an example of the cultural tensions presented by George Ritzer in his 1993 book, *The McDonaldization of Society?* In comparison with the evident ability of the spontaneous, do-it-yourself spirituality of the street to speak to the human condition, and provide useful vehicles for the expression of emotions of all kinds, did the inherited western Christian ways of handling crisis look too much like 'McDoctrine' – a spiritual fast-food of proof-texts and clichés that (like their culinary equivalent) might seem filling and fattening in the normal flow of everyday life (at least for those accustomed to such a diet), but which in the larger context of cosmic tragedy appeared, at best, to be irrelevant and simplistic?

Again, this can be related back to precedents in Diana's life, for she had often been portrayed as antithetical to the western rationalized tradition which she inherited, and which in turn had victimized her through its unyielding protocol, undergirded by appeals to some notion of universal reason. In struggling with these opposing ways of being, she herself had regularly indulged in spontaneous, do-it-yourself spirituality and, like many of her mourners, she sought to create a relevant personal path by utilizing ancient ingredients in the reinvention of a meaningful spirituality for our day. Dunblane evoked very similar themes, particularly in relation to the ages of the murdered children, who were frequently referred to as angels, their connection to the spiritual realm often seeming to be in inverse proportion to their corruption by the rationalizing forces which again had been responsible for their tragic end.

The tactile and symbolic

Another prominent factor was the intuitive utilization of tactile and symbolic ways of accessing reality. This relates directly to the pilgrimage theme, for on a pilgrimage the various elements that are common to all the pilgrims (clothes, songs, and so on) 'create a sacred atmosphere that intensifies sensitivity to the symbols that compose it'. Symbols have the power to deal with a sense of experienced powerlessness: the very least they do is to give people a feeling that they know what they are doing, and are actually in control of a situation that otherwise seems chaotic. In life, people flocked to see Diana, taking her gifts, and expecting her to respond and change things (which she evidently did). Was the throwing of flowers at her coffin an expression of the same hope? The fundamental relationship between everyday spirituality, symbols and tactile experiences is one of the universal aspects of being human, and is a key way in which oral peoples have traditionally handled pain and discontinuity. One of the major ironies of our situation today is that western culture is rapidly reverting to the characteristics of an oral culture which many thought had disappeared for good. Though we have high levels of literacy, increasing numbers even of educated middle-class people choose to adopt a lifestyle of functional illiteracy, and in this situation the adequacy of faith will be judged not on the basis of intellectual discourse, but by its capacity to help people get through the night and then wake to new possibilities in the morning. This way of being has largely disappeared from the horizons of western Christianity, being either ignored altogether or dismissed as unchristian superstition. In consequence, we find it difficult, if not impossible, to forge meaningful connections between revealed aspects of faith and the use of mythical, a-historical and archetypal images to connect with the meaning of life in the context of a wider cosmos.

The power of stories

When analytical theological discourse fails because we are faced with questions to which there is no obvious answer, nor even an appropriate response in terms of the rules of reason and logic, stories are a key source of healing. In the mourning relating to both Dunblane and Diana, telling stories played a huge part in helping people to deal with the horror of what had happened. I was myself caught up in the aftermath of the Dunblane tragedy, and telling the story of people I met, things that took place, both in my church and in the wider community, became a way of coping. Others found that the events of those days evoked hidden memories of chance encounters with the children who died, with their parents – even with the gunman himself – and while these were often painful recollections, the sharing of them became a kind of corporate therapy. After Diana's death, people recalled how they, or someone they knew, had met her in unexpected situations, received a visit or a letter from her, or had been otherwise inspired by her example. Telling stories was a way to carry on, while also moving beyond mere survival into a celebration of the strength of the human spirit. In both cases, this ongoing telling of stories has taken on an almost sacramental flavour, undergirded by the need to remember, not allowing the memory to falter. The release of CDs, the wearing of ribbons, even the purchase of souvenirs, all fulfil this basic need. Moreover, this is a redemptive need, for by buying these items, or making donations to trust funds, people with no stories of their own identify themselves with the bigger story. It is easy to be cynical about some of this, but underlying it all is a genuine desire on the part of many people to see things change for the better. They want to have a stake in the bigger meta-narrative, because that opens up the possibility of redemption, not only for others, but frequently for themselves too. It is a cliché to say that people can never be the same after tragedy strikes, but in these cases that is more true of more people than we sometimes imagine. The existing prior identification of Diana as in some sense a redemptive person herself merely highlighted the potentially redemptive nature of the grieving pilgrimages, something that will no doubt continue through pilgrimage to her grave and the Althorp estate.

The grand vision

In the midst of all this – and contrary to all the predictions of postmodern theorists – there has undoubtedly surfaced a renewed search for some meta-narrative that will put these fragments of human experience into a wider context. The human spirit has a constant need for value-communicating myths, and these events have provided a particularly powerful one. In a culture struggling with the reality of post-Nazi humanism which seemed to extinguish for ever the possibility that human endeavour could by itself get things right and embody the divine, the events following Dunblane and Diana in particular have pushed some central archetypal buttons in people's corporate psyche.

To put a Christian spin on it, has 'From Dunblane to Diana' become 'From the Massacre of the Innocents to the Crucifixion-and Beyond'? Over the last two decades, Hollywood movies have made us increasingly expectant of the intervention of external figures who will bring redemptive answers from beyond ourselves. The Dunblane children were – and still are – regularly referred to as angels. Did Diana in death embody even more powerfully the elusive possibility that we (or someone like us) might yet break through and be both human and divine? In a site on the worldwide web entitled 'Forever Young', the claim is made that 'Never in the history of the world has the death of one individual affected so many people...'

Whether or not the Christocentric overtones were intended, that seems to be the context in which much of the post-Diana rhetoric is most readily located. Consider the following correspondences between the story of Diana and the story of Christ:

- She came from humble and/or obscure origins, and her true significance was appreciated only when it was too late.
- She was an outsider in the world in which she operated.
- She was a person of special compassion, concerned for children, the meek and oppressed, the afflicted and the powerless – because she was one of them.
- She had access to special powers, based on different standards than most of us adopt in everyday life. She brought about 'miracles' of healing, lifting up those at the very edges of society (AIDS victims, lepers, those disfigured by land mines), and displayed unique gifts serving the cause of truth and justice, apparently able to harness the energies of the rich and powerful to causes that they would otherwise not have supported. She was a new kind of 'star child', capable of changing the unchangeable.
- She was opposed by the ideological power-brokers of the day – able to save others, but ultimately not able to save herself.
- She was hunted down by the agents of authority (paparazzi et al.), in life and even to the point of death.
- She died a very public, very cruel, lingering death, which left her innate beauty disfigured and her body physically broken.
- She was laid to rest in a completely new grave site, never before used for that purpose.

Moreover, no leaps of imagination are required to trace such correspondences, for all these and more are explicitly spelled out in Elton John's song 'Candle in the Wind', as also in the funeral oration delivered by Diana's brother, Earl Spencer. There are some things missing from this checklist, of course. Because this is real-life, and not the Hollywood special-effects department, there is – so far – no resurrection, and no eternal presence. But recall what happened after the death of Elvis Presley in 1977 – and watch this space! And, from the point of view of Christian witness, consider the clear connection between these themes and the Christ figure of the New Testament. To what extent does John 1:11 provide a fitting epitaph for Diana? 'She came to the world that was her own, but her own people did not accept her. Yet to all who did accept and believe, she gave the right to become children of God.' And what does that mean in terms of the church's mission? Much more work needs to be done before an answer to that can adequately be teased out. This is not the place to pursue it further, except to note that in terms of the church's mission, the similarities between these two great archetypal stories are something that the church cannot afford to ignore.

Understanding the cultural context

There will be no shortage of commentators making a superficial link between all this and the much-discussed paradigm shift from modernity to postmodernity. But determining the exact relationship between these trends is more complex than merely putting a label on it all. In particular, it does make a difference whether the Diana phenomenon was a unique experience, unlikely to be repeated, or whether it is the latest episode in a significant nascent form of popular spiritual expression. I wish to suggest that it is the latter. Without (I hope) being pretentious about it, I would argue that the mourning for Diana was an entirely predictable outcome of the trends that I had myself noted in my book *Faith in a Changing Culture*, published only four months before her death. In spite of that, I was still taken by surprise when it all happened, for two reasons. First, one rarely gets such outstanding empirical support for one's theories about spirituality and mission so soon after putting them forward. And secondly, I had accepted the conclusions of those sociologists who had argued that historical antecedents such as the Anfield pilgrimage (following the Hillsborough football stadium disaster) were a localised phenomenon entirely contingent on the culture of Merseyside. Dunblane ought to have alerted me to the fact that this was part of a pattern of massive cultural change, though once again there were what looked like special local factors, particularly the Scottish dimension and the kind of close-knit community that was involved. However, I believe we can now see a clear trend linking all the recent examples of public grief, but especially Anfield-Dunblane-Diana, and see them as symptomatic of the shift from modernity to post-modernity. As such, they are of interest not only to cultural analysts, but also – and especially – to the churches in relation to their missionary task.

Furthermore, they help to locate what post-modernity might mean in relation to the church's mission. In particular, they give support for the opinion that people are, for the most part, 'post-modern' in a sociological sense rather than ideologically 'postmodern' in terms of their worldview. The way in which people handled Diana's death – particularly the underlying implied search for new self-created meta-narratives – supports the opinion that the end of our cultural love-affair with modernity has come about more on pragmatic grounds than as a result of philosophical principle. The search for new ways of being is driven by forces that are 'post-modern' (where the hyphen indicates something emerging 'after' the 'modern' ways of doing things have outlived their usefulness), rather than by the nostrums of 'postmodernism' in the ideological sense. Popular culture (as distinct, perhaps, from academic or intellectual culture) has not adopted some grand philosophical vision, but is simply aware of the deficiencies of inherited ways of doing things, foremost among which is a sense that the Enlightenment worldview has led to an unhealthy dismissal of the relevance of anything spiritual, and that the church – far from being the solution – is actually part of the problem. This in turn sheds further light on how the church can be in such serious decline at a time when the culture is far more openly religious or spiritual than it has been for some considerable time. Could it be that, by its uncritical embracing of the culture of modernity, not only did the church historically accept some notions that were actually

Christian heresies, but it also embraced the methods of modernity to such an extent that, at least in the West, Christians do not know how to contextualize the gospel in a different cultural frame of reference? Dean W. R. Inge (1860-1954) is credited with having observed that a church married to the spirit of one age will find itself widowed in the next. Is the church's predicament less a crisis of religion or spirituality, and more a crisis of culture, stemming from the fact that at a time when fewer and fewer people still find meaning within the culture of modernity, that is the only culture in which the church knows how to operate?

Challenges for the churches

Related to this cultural challenge, we can also trace several specific issues that have been highlighted by recent events. This is not an exhaustive list, nor is it possible to do any more than summarize them briefly.

The creation of a 'non-religious' image for the church

At a time when politics is increasingly regarded as a power struggle among diverse interest groups, the churches are easily perceived as just another pressure group. Ironically, this seems to have been encouraged by the churches' own self-conscious engagement with social and political issues, for perfectly good and justifiable reasons, both theological and strategic. Though this was the last thing that was ever intended, the resultant image can be one of a church which is 'unspiritual', more interested in the material than in the religious – and for that reason, no more (or less) deserving of being taken seriously than any other special interest group in society. Encouraging this perception is the ready acceptance of an 'establishment' image, which inevitably means that when commitment to other institutions with their base in modernity diminishes, the church is bound to feel the impact. I would be the last to argue for a separation of mission and social action – indeed, I see them as two sides of the same coin – but for that very reason we need to work at ensuring that we develop a holistic understanding of faith, in which the spiritual is no less central than the material.

Perpetuation of an exclusively cognitive culture

The extent to which this is the case varies from one Christian tradition to another, though it is generally true that, to cope with church, people need to be able to process abstract concepts through their mental processes, and those who more naturally deal with things in an intuitive, artistic, or creative way will find little that speaks to them. On the whole, today's Christians tend to prefer the propositional, and express varying degrees of uneasiness with image, symbols, and particularly the imagination. This is true even of those traditions which have been most historically rooted in a more visual and interactive spirituality. We need a renewed theology of the human person and of spiritual growth.

Embarrassment with the mystical, the numinous, and the spiritual

Western Christians have not only bought into a cognitive culture, but one dominated by rationalism and materialism. There is significant embarrassment about such things as angels, heaven, the after-life, and so on. At best, the church seems to speak uncomfortably of them – at worst, it gives the impression that it no longer believes in them. All this makes us look oddly out of tune with a world that sometimes seems interested in nothing else. One of the greatest ironies of the twentieth century is the way that in the 1920s and 1930s, Protestant theologians were falling over themselves to 'demythologize' the gospel, at exactly the moment that Einstein was inaugurating the move towards a 'remythologized' scientific paradigm. We are still struggling with the consequences of that.

Issues of control, power and patriarchy

To a greater degree than most of us would like to acknowledge, the inherited organizational and theological styles of all our churches find their roots in the patriarchal culture of the British empire (and, beyond that, back to ancient Rome). Not only has this led to many people feeling marginalized by the churches, but it has also nurtured an unhealthy domination of Christian thinking by an essentially heretical view of God, deriving from Greek philosophy, in which all our theological outcomes need to be 'successful', and there is little or no space for tragedy and suffering, or for emotions like grief and failure. Alongside this is a deep-seated unwillingness to allow – still less empower – those who are not the 'right' people, to construct their own do-it-yourself theology and spirituality. This is a major issue, for central to all the events mentioned here has been a form of spirituality and worship that grows from the grass roots up, rather than being imposed from the top down. Theologians and church leaders readily articulate the need for a servant church, but to put that into practice means that we ought to be providing the infrastructure of spirituality, not its superstructure. How and what to build on that infrastructure will then be the responsibility of the individual, and facing that responsibility is a key component of what gives life its spiritual meaning.

I am aware of having stated the issues somewhat starkly here: it would certainly be appropriate to debate the various nuances of what I am claiming. But the key missiological issue is not so much whether all this is true in the absolute sense, but whether it approximates to people's perceptions of the church – and on the whole I believe it does.

Revisiting the key themes

This is not the place for an exhaustive exposition of how Christians might engage creatively with the renewed popular spirituality of our day. Still, it will be worth drawing attention to the fact that there are significant spiritual riches within the

Christian tradition at precisely those points that I have argued were central to what took place post-Dunblane and in the wake of Diana's death.

Pilgrimage

The role of pilgrimage in the Bible is obvious. It occurs everywhere as a key image for the understanding of faith, whether in relation to the literal visiting of places, or in historical episodes such as the Passover and Exodus traditions, or the symbolic enactment of such historical moments in the worship of the Jerusalem temple. In addition, the language of pilgrimage is frequently used in a metaphorical way to refer to faith as a journey. Protestants in particular have generally felt happier with the individualistic and internalized understanding of pilgrimage classically presented in Bunyan's *Pilgrim's Progress*, rather than the tangible, experiential, moving pilgrimage reflected in the models of worship presented in the Bible and continued in the original architectural intent of many ancient church buildings, with their open spaces within which processionals and other forms of movement were a good deal easier to orchestrate than they would be in today's churches, with their clutter of furniture. Does the church have something to relearn and rediscover here? We should not underestimate the extent to which this may be threatening for some, as pilgrimage embodies an understanding of faith that is dynamic, growing, provisional, and evolving – in stark contrast to the models of faith inherited from modernity, where everything had to be rationalized, predictable, commodified, and neatly definable.

Spontaneity

For similar reasons, the church is often afraid of spontaneity, of allowing people to create their own spiritual spaces and formulate their own expressions of faith. Who knows what might happen when the 'wrong' sort of people get their hands on matters that hitherto have been the preserve of those with the 'right' sort of training, and the approval and authorization of the regular institutional structures? That question is easily answered, for that is precisely what has happened among many groups of non-western Christians, often under the leadership of women and children, not to mention the downtrodden and oppressed – and the result has been massive growth of the church to a point where, in world terms, white western Christians are now outnumbered by others two to one. At a time when British churches face serious decline, only a fool could imagine that we have nothing to learn from this, though it cannot be denied that any learning might have to be at the expense of some of our most cherished notions. In spontaneous spirituality, creeds are likely to be less important than autobiography and the shared search for meaning, and the rediscovery of praxis as a key expression of faith will challenge the inherited supremacy of rationality over experience.

The tactile and symbolic

Perhaps nothing goes so directly to the heart of much of our present predicament. Theologically, there is a challenge here to our apparent inability – or unwillingness – to engage with the question of formulating a creation-centred spirituality which will be able to embrace both the historical Jesus and the cosmic Christ or, to express it differently, the relationship between the cognitive and the affective. Ironically, there is no shortage of material for bridging this gap within the Christian tradition, for while the (cognitive) understanding of the Bible has always been central for theologians, for most Christians throughout most of history, regular devotion has needed to focus on other forms of spirituality, for the simple reason that they have been illiterate. Mosaics, painting, stained glass, statues, carvings, music, and other artistic and symbolic expressions of meaning were natural components of a holistic spirituality that touched all the senses of smell, touch, vision, hearing, and so on. Just as the divine word became flesh through the incarnation, so the Bible and its message was incarnated and made accessible to the wider population through the use of relevant images, most of which were both tactile and symbolic. The use of literature goes right back to the first generation of the church, and when the Reformers found themselves in a situation where the printed book was emerging as a medium of mass-communication, they naturally contextualized the gospel within that culture. Unfortunately, subsequent generations have not been so perceptive, and even today some Christians do not appreciate that the traditional book-based era is coming to an end. Under the mistaken belief that the only way to preserve the integrity of the divine word must be through a cognitive, propositional, book-centred understanding of faith, Christians have effectively left the new visual and tactile image-making machine of the twentieth century to search for its own values with which to portray and understand the human condition. In the process, the word has not become flesh, but has been reimprisoned in words – something that is not only bad communication strategy, but bad theology as well, for it is in effect a heretical denial of the incarnation. The notion that only things with a cognitive and rational base can be meaningful is not true either to human nature or to the gospel. Oral cultures have always had a holistic foundation, endowing all of life with spiritual meaning – and usually making that connection through the use of symbols and ritual. In the post-modern context (which has more similarities with oral cultures than most observers will admit), these are the things that will deepen faith and bring life into harmony with belief. These are also the very things that western theism has generally devalued, but which will need to be rediscovered if there is to be an effective Christian witness in the new context. In a recent book Clark Pinnock – hardly at the radical end of the theological spectrum – concludes: 'We do ourselves harm when we eliminate arts, drama, color, vestments, pageantry, incense, saints, calendars, lectionary, sculpture.'

The power of stories

In his book *Generation X*, based on the imaginary conversations of three friends who opt out of the mainstream to live in the Arizona desert, Douglas Coupland observes that '...it's not healthy to live life as a succession of isolated little cool moments. Either our lives become stories, or there's just no way to get through them... this is why the three of us left our lives behind us and came to the desert – to tell stories and to make our own lives worthwhile tales in the process.' Later on, he admits that '...most of us have only two or three genuinely interesting moments in our lives, the rest is filler... at the end of our lives most of us will be lucky if any of those moments connect together to form a story that anyone would find remotely interesting.' Even Hollywood has called the Bible 'The Greatest Story Ever Told' and, like the stories told around the tragedies of Dunblane and Diana, it is a story with a redemptive purpose. Telling the stories of faith, relating them to our own personal stories, discovering new images of Christ that will speak with power to today's generation, may lead to a more open-ended sharing of faith than some Christians will be happy with. But the very fact that stories leave spaces for meanings, and create new possibilities for the exploration of spirituality, means that they will more effectively address the concerns of everyday life, cross cultural boundaries, and invite the active participation and commitment of those who share in their telling.

The grand vision

Douglas Coupland, to whom I have just referred, is one of the most perceptive observers of the spirituality of our age. In his book *Life after God*, at the end of 300 pages of stories expressing the plight of what he calls 'the first generation raised without religion', he finds himself in the quietness of a temperate rain forest in his native British Columbia, about to plunge into a cool stream of water where he hopes to find a fresh angle on life and its meaning. 'Now – here is my secret', he writes, 'I tell it to you with an openness of heart that I doubt I shall ever achieve again, so I pray that you are in a quiet room as you hear these words. My secret is that I need God – that I am sick and can no longer make it alone. I need God to help me give, because I no longer seem capable of giving; to help me be kind, as I no longer seem capable of kindness; to help me love, as I seem beyond being able to love.' At a time when many others are openly echoing his words, the church often seems to be enmeshed in its own trivialities, and to those outside presents itself as having lost its own grand vision – the foundational Biblical vision of a world in which God is at work, together with the apostolic vision of how the innate spiritual search of humanity can be a pointer towards the gospel. The events of recent years have provided several such signs. What we need now are Christians with the vision, the spirituality, the humanity and the compassion to know how to utilize them effectively.

DIANA, QUEEN OF HEARTS

Mourning and social solidarity

Tony Walter

Saint DIANA
THE IRREPLACEABLE PATRON SAINT OF LOVE
In Our Hearts Forever

T his message, written in red and black felt-tip pen on a large
yellow card, was one of the thousands pinned to the railings
near Kensington Palace. Two others nearby read 'The Princess of
Wales to Royalty, but The Queen of Hearts to The Commoners'
and 'WE WILL ALWAYS LOVE YOU DIANA'. All three notices
were adorned with red hearts. Among the millions of messages
pinned to railings and flowers world-wide and written in books of
condolence, many portrayed Diana as the embodiment of
compassion and love, a caring person who in turn evoked love
from others (including the writers of the messages).

I am in no position to judge Princess Diana's actual qualities
of compassion or lack of them. She was surely as complex and
contradictory as any human being, on the one hand going down
to Centrepoint to give soup to the homeless in the middle of the
night without seeking any press attention, on the other hand
driving recklessly (on more than one occasion) in order to get
away from photographers without any apparent concern that her
children might be left motherless. Who knows where she would
come in a world league of compassion? What this chapter
explores, however, is why she has the very epitome of love and
compassion. Why should a probably fairly ordinary human
being (living, admittedly, an extraordinary life) have been so
speedily beatified? And why in 1997 should the British have been
so keen to elevate her into a symbol of compassion? In this
chapter, I will discuss three possible explanations.

The royal touch

In many cultures around the world, royal personages are believed to link earth and heaven. They are ordinary mortals, yet are perceived as totally other, partaking in the divine. Their ability to mediate between heaven and earth is often reflected in their special healing powers. For example, during the Middle Ages, it was widely believed that those who suffered from scrofula, a glandular disease, could be cured by being touched by their monarch. This belief in the 'royal touch', as it was called, lasted from the time of Edward the Confessor right up to 1714, when Queen Anne performed the last royal touch. In France, the other country where this belief was held, the last royal touch was performed in 1825, by Charles X. Some English monarchs took their responsibilities seriously, others thought the whole thing a nonsense. Elizabeth I, for example, seldom performed the ceremony, whereas Charles II is reported to have touched nearly 100,000 people between the time of his restoration and his death. It is remarkable to think that people in England believed in the power of touch for almost 700 years, and that generation after generation went to see their monarch in order to be cured.

I am sure that Diana's touch, and her look, did have healing power. If I were lying sick with AIDS or leprosy in a hospital bed and the most beautiful woman in the world came to visit me, held my hand, gazed at me with those huge eyes, and gave me unconditional positive regard, I am sure I'd feel a lot better! In visiting the sick, Diana was merely playing the required role of a British royal, but by all accounts she did it particularly well, putting all of herself into it rather than seeing it as just a duty. Some have suggested that her own experience of abandonment gave her a very real fellow feeling for the rejected, as her brother suggested in his funeral speech.

Be that as it may, the question remains, why should Diana's 'royal touch' have meant so much to so many millions who had not met her? Why should this have struck such a chord in Britain at this time? Royals have been touching and healing for centuries, so why was it so important in 1997? To answer this question, we have to look at the next two possible explanations.

The good rich girl

In an article published on October 2nd, Ross McKibbin made the important point that Diana was mourned most in Britain and the USA. Any explanation of the massive response to her death has to take into account both that it was global, and that it was particularly pronounced in these two particular countries. Any explanation that sees the mourning as uniformly global, or just Anglo-American, cannot be correct.

So what is it about the USA and the UK? McKibbin notes that they are the major western countries in which social solidarity is at its weakest, and in this he is correct. Both countries have for centuries been more individualistic than most, with the USA in particular being notorious for celebrating the individual more than social solidarity. In the UK, the post-1979 Thatcher era consciously promoted values of individual responsibility over mutual responsibility one for another, and certainly over responsibility of the State for the well-being of its citizens, thus undermining the post-war consensus over the welfare state. Both Thatcher and Reagan rated personal acts of charity more highly than state-provided welfare. As McKibbin puts it, in this view 'The remedy for social failure, poverty or homelessness is to be found in individual virtue'.

Britons and Americans have absorbed nearly twenty years of this rhetoric and many have come to believe it, so they warmed to Princess Diana's acts of charity. She shows us that you can be extremely rich and yet remain a good person, a far more comfortable message than Mother Teresa's message that goodness entails possessing just a bucket and one sari. No wonder millions found more hope in Diana than in Mother Teresa, especially in those countries that celebrate getting rich quick plus personal charity. No wonder she went down well in Hollywood. To the extent that the market economics and slimmed-down state welfare promoted by Thatcher have now influenced almost the entire world, one might expect a certain response to Diana's death in other countries too, as indeed was the case.

If this is why people promoted Diana to patron saint of love, then it is an intensely depressing explanation, certainly for those like me to the left of centre. As Michael Billig, put it, 'royalty are recruited as publicised figureheads to encourage others to give from their less substantial resources: even the poorest are donors.' But there is a third, more hopeful, explanation.

Embodied love

This third explanation sees the response to Diana not as an expression of Thatcherite market values but as a rejection of them. In promoting the idea that the impersonal market will solve most social problems, Thatcher abandoned the rhetoric of a caring society that had marked her predecessors (both Conservative and Labour). Previous leaders had stated that society should be caring as well as economically efficient. Add to this new political rhetoric the Windsors, a family that certainly had deeply held moral concerns, but that increasingly appeared unfeeling, and we have in the UK a society driven by economic rationality with nobody at the top expressing or embodying those other virtues that are needed for a society to cohere and be a decent place in which to live.

The mid 1980s witnessed a motley array of personalities who, briefly, entered the limelight as expressing the human compassion that seemed absent at the formal level of national leadership. In 1984, Bob Geldof's visit to Ethiopia and the Live Aid concert filled the vacuum; then the Church of England's 1985 report Faith in the City briefly articulated the compassion and social justice that was so strikingly absent at the level of political rhetoric; even Prince Charles for a while held out visions of a more caring, greener, more sustainable society. But by the late 1980s and 1990s, Diana had evolved from shy, pretty young princess through queen of fashion into 'the wounded healer', the glamorous princess who touched lepers and those with AIDS yet who was herself vulnerable. Most important, she didn't just talk about compassion, she literally embodied it. Capturing those photogenic eyes and her ability physically to touch and hold those in pain, countless photographs of Diana with the sick and the rejected showed a woman at the very highest level embodying precisely those virtues so hard to discern in other political and royal leaders. She embodied all the virtues denied by economic rationality and political calculation. She acted, she said, simply from the heart.

So, I would suggest Diana was mourned most in Britain (or was it mainly England, mentally far more Thatcherite than Scotland and Wales?) and the USA because it is in these countries self-interest and profit have been most successfully preached. People loved Diana because she rejected these values, not because she expressed them.

The politics of compassion

Which of these last two explanations is correct? What happened a few weeks later at the annual party political conferences is significant. Clearly, the Tories (who had in May catastrophically lost the general election) thought the mourning for Diana was a judgement on them, while Labour saw it as vindicating their own approach. So, at the Conservative Party conference we find the two 'hardest' men of the old Tory regime admitting:

'Our reputation has suffered because we failed to wear our hearts on our sleeves'. (Michael Portillo)

'It's to do with language... After eighteen years the people got fed up with our language'. (Michael Howard)

'Hague seeks the party that cares' announced *The Times* in its front page headline, after the new Conservative leader's speech. The mourning for Diana confirmed what Conservatives had already diagnosed as the reason for their electoral failure, namely that they had appeared uncaring. Meanwhile, Labour were quietly gloating.

Mr Blair avoided mentioning Diana, Princess of Wales, believing it to be inappropriate, but his speech was peppered with references to the new compassionate spirit abroad in Britain, and to a 'quiet revolution' taking place. He sensed 'confidence returning to the British people, compassion to the British soul, unity to the British nation'. His ambition was a compassionate society, but it was 'compassion with a hard edge, because a strong society could not be built on soft choices'.

Whether Blair's subsequent policies will, or will not, further a compassionate society is an open question. My point is that the political rhetoric has changed, and that politicians on both sides identify Diana with Labour's rhetoric of a compassionate society, not with the Tory rhetoric of market forces plus private charity. It seems then that politicians on both sides thought Diana represented popular judgement on Thatcherism, not an endorsement of it.

Of course, few if any of the messages of condolence mentioned Thatcher or her successor John Major. Many identified the Windsors as their object of criticism, and this is to be expected. It was, after all, the Windsors and not Thatcher with whom Diana had found herself in personal conflict.

The long-term test will be whether the British (or American) people show a willingness to pay higher taxes in order to fund an improved welfare state. Will charities find there are more and more volunteers, especially for the kind of unfashionable causes Diana sponsored? Will the millions of words of compassion spoken and written in September 1977 become converted into true acts of compassion? At this point, a fourth possibility emerges, which combines the second and third possibilities. It seems as though many people in Britain do want a more caring society, only they want it without sacrifice. The Labour Party promised a fairer, more caring Britain, without raising taxes.

The British seem to want goodness and 'caring' without hard choices: the NHS, but low – or preferably no – taxes; better working conditions, but no trades unions; fair shares and better times for all, but no redistribution of wealth; a society stripped of deference, but *Hello!* magazine wall-to-wall. Grief for Diana expressed that perfectly. You could emote all you wanted without having to give anything up.

Gender, power and suffering

There is a gender element to all this. So far, I have suggested Diana was a symbol of compassion in a world gone mad with money-making, a symbol of acting from the heart in world obsessed with calculating rationality. But she was also a woman. A few weeks after her death, at the MTV Video Music Award, The Spice Girls, wearing black armbands, spoke about the princess' 'formidable girl power'. Unlike the Queen and unlike Thatcher, Diana represented the powerful woman who is not de-sexed, one who embodied feminine values of the heart without appearing weak or dependent. Though despised by many intellectuals, Diana and The Spice Girls may have appealed to the masses for similar reasons. Diana's 'heart' highlighted the inadequacies not only of male rationalities, but also of feminist rationalities, without reverting to the powerlessness of the pre-feminist woman.

Some feminist and Marxist writers have been appalled at the sanctification of vulnerability and suffering that appears to lie at the heart of Diana's attraction for many. It seems to me that there is a basic divide here. On the one hand there are those, including many from the Christian tradition, who can see purpose in the strong becoming weak and identifying with the weak. On the other hand, there are those, including some feminists and most Marxists, who see hope only in the weak recognizing their strength and empowering themselves. Responses to Diana's death clearly revealed this split over the value of suffering.

The re-creation of society

Throughout history, mourning has been one of the major sources of social solidarity. I think of a friend whose father died when he was fifteen. For the three weeks after his death, he and his sister and mother slept in the same room, expressing a primordial need to cling together with others at the time when the family was threatened by one of its members being torn from its midst. At the beginning of this century, the French sociologist Emile Durkheim, who argued that religion is rooted in group solidarity, based his thesis on studies of Aboriginal religious rituals, many of which were rituals of mourning. When a group loses a member, it gathers together in rituals to reaffirm that the group will survive. As another sociologist put it 'Every human society is, in the last resort, men banded together in the face of death.'

The group that bands together is the group that has been attacked by death – in Aboriginal society a hunting group, more typically in the modern West a nuclear family. Just occasionally, the person who dies represents something much bigger, as when President John Kennedy was shot in 1963. The presidency, like the flag, represents the entire American nation. Quite who and what Diana represented will long be a matter of debate, but it is clear that her death affected millions. The result was that millions banded together in the face of her death, though the original impulse may have been for individual families to band together as they travelled up to London with their flowers and their messages. But the result was the spectacle of society banded together. Fifteen or so years earlier, Margaret Thatcher had announced that 'There is no such thing as society, only individuals and families'. In 1997 in the royal parks of London and in the cyberspace of electronic condolence, the society that Thatcher said did not exist was symbolically reconstituted. A huge Union Jack draped outside Kensington Palace had inscribed upon it 'God's United Kingdom'.

At the level of rhetoric, Thatcherism was finally silenced in 1997. First in the landslide Labour victory of May, and then in the mourning for Diana. I am not alone in making connections between the sense of euphoria in May and in September. Both occasions witnessed the unusual phenomenon of strangers conversing on the

London underground. Somehow there was a sense that, once again, we can be a society, not just fragmented individuals.

But, and this is a huge but, all this occurred at the level of ritual and of rhetoric. People cannot live day-by-day as they do during ritual and worship. As the anthropologist Victor Turner observes, the social function of ritual is to articulate values, especially those of equality and solidarity, that cannot pervade everyday life, and by articulating them to challenge everyday life. Ritual behaviour reveals another way of relating. In Saint Augustine's terms it reveals the City of God to the City of Men. Ritual and everyday life, at best, live in creative tension with one another. At the time of writing (April 1998), I very much doubt that Britain has become a much more compassionate society, nor that the Labour government's policies are likely to promote such a society, but the rhetoric, the vision, has changed. The values by which our leaders are judged have changed. And Diana and her death may prove no small part of that shift of vision.

Louise Woodward

The solidarity expressed in Diana's mourning was also totalitarian, silencing those many who did not mourn. This is perfectly normal in societies where there is socially imposed mourning: dissident individuals just have to shut up and put up. But the signs became ominous a month later. The human interest story that eventually pushed Diana off the front pages was the trial a month later of the British au pair Louise Woodward, tried for the murder of the baby in her care in Massachusetts. Here was another nineteen year old (the same age that Diana married), out of her depth in a family that used her. The 'free Louise Woodward' lobby, fuelled by English nationalism and with no evidence other than their own intuition, simply could not believe this young English girl abroad could be a murderess. Any English person who suggested otherwise had to shut up and put up, just as a month before. Whether the new solidarity born in the UK in 1997 is one we can be proud of, only time will tell.

Death of a Princess

58

LOST WITHOUT HER SOUL?

Diana and the search for transcendence

David Hilborn

Like Diana, the novelist Douglas Coupland was born in 1961. All Coupland's books reflect the struggle of his and Diana's generation for what he has called 'transcendence' and 'epiphany'. Common though these terms are in traditional Christianity, Coupland applies them to something altogether more diffuse and eclectic. Not least in his bestseller *Life After God*, he meditates on a widespread 'sickness' suffered by twenty and thirtysomethings in the West today. This sickness comes from a profound spiritual dislocation – from the experience of having abandoned orthodox faith and church allegiance, while nonetheless still yearning for ultimate meaning and supernatural insight. He writes of his contemporaries as those who have settled for a post-Christian life of 'earthly salvation', and yet insists in the same breath that 'we are living creatures – we have religious impulses – we must'. He then asks a question which goes to heart of what happened in the first week of September 1997 – the week following Diana's death: 'And yet into what cracks do these impulses flow in a world without religion? It is something I think about every day. Sometimes I think it is the only thing I should be thinking about.'

Diana herself had plenty of 'religious impulses'. But like Coupland and his friends, she found it difficult to channel them. Rather, they flowed into a diverse range of 'cracks' – from astrology to charity work, from Eastern mysticism to colonic irrigation, from spiritism to psychotherapy, from aristocratic Anglicanism through Roman Catholicism to Islam. In this sense, she personified the characteristic movement of contemporary western spirituality away from established religious institutions and towards a search for 'transcendence' and 'epiphany' which is at once more idiosyncratic, more plural and more provisional.

On the internet, there used to be a web site devoted exclusively to Diana's star chart. Morbidly, for months after the tragedy in Paris, it continued to display readings not only for the date of Diana's death, but for several days beyond it. The Princess' entry for Sunday August 31st carried no hint of impending doom; no dark portent of disaster; no veiled warning to stay indoors and avoid danger. In fact, the advice given to Diana for what turned out to be her dying day was very positive. Indeed, it focused poignantly on her spiritual life: 'Your psychic sensitivity and intuition', it declared, 'are heightened at this time… you are fired up about your ideals and can stir others to action.' By Monday September 1st Diana's body had been flown back to Britain from Paris, but until recently you could still surf onto her forecast for that day, too: 'The world of mysticism is very appealing to you now', it said, 'and if you have talent in [this area] it could be a very fruitful time for you.'

In Andrew Morton's biography, transcripts of Diana's interviews for the author contain several references to astrology: to a consultation in 1984 when the planets apparently confirmed her hunch that she would never be Queen, and to in-depth sessions with the celebrity stargazers Penny Thornton and Debbie Frank.

But as her starcharts themselves acknowledged, astrology provided only one of several outlets for Diana's 'religious impulses'. Indeed, she was far from exclusive about any particular route into 'transcendence' or 'epiphany'. Rather, like so many of her generation, she preferred to keep her options open on such matters. By all accounts, she was a 'seeker' who never quite found the 'answer' to life. She travelled along a whole range of spiritual, psychological and emotional paths. So from time to time she also consulted a clairvoyant who, in her own words, had helped her contact a deceased grandmother, a long-lamented uncle and a former police bodyguard. Then there was tai-chi, which she took to in the early '90s with great zeal, not to mention a panoply of alternative therapists and counsellors to ease her through her chronic bulimia and her desperately sad suicide attempts. Even in her post-divorce years, when she became more confident and self-sufficient, Morton recounts 'weekly trips to see her therapist Susie Orbach at her North London home, and what [the Princess] herself called "Pamper Diana" days, when she enjoyed a variety of New Age [treatments]'. As Diana herself once said of her diverse spiritual explorations, 'I've got a lot to learn. I've got 101 books sitting by books – piles of books. [I'm] absolutely gripped.'

Diana's multi-track pilgrimage is characteristic of much in contemporary western spirituality. More specifically it can be taken to typify what has come to be called 'postmodern spirituality'. Since, however, 'postmodern spirituality' is a phrase more often used than explained, I shall start with some definitions.

Spirituality

The word 'spirituality' does not enter the vocabulary of western Christian culture in any significant way until the nineteenth century. According to the Oxford Catholic theologian Simon Tugwell, its use in this context is recent, while more confident use of the term is very recent indeed. It is only in the past century that 'spirituality' has been developed as a distinct 'compartment' of western religious life – a separate category of sacred devotion to be practised and studied in its own right, apart from the doctrine, liturgy, and history of the Church. In his fine anthology of post-war spirituality, John Garvey puts this separation down to the growth of what he calls 'the secular point of view' during the same period. He notes, 'It is hard to imagine the use of a word like "spirituality" by Maximus the Confessor or one of the Fathers or Mothers of the Desert, who didn't think they were talking about a category called spirituality but rather about the way the souls of human beings work – about the most basic human truths.'

By contrast, the pursuit of 'spiritual' truth today has shifted significantly from the public square into the private sphere of individual experience and personal choice. As a result, it has taken on a life, and identity, of its own. The increased secularism to which Garvey refers has internalised the quest of the soul. It has also opened up a division between the 'official' spiritualities of mainline religious traditions and the 'self-made' spiritualities of those many who still profess faith in God, but who do so apart from the church, the synagogue, the mosque or the temple. This is partly what the sociologist Grace Davie means when she summarises the religious climate of post-war Britain in the phrase 'believing without belonging'. It is a phrase borne out by statistics. Church membership in the UK has fallen from around half the population in the mid-1800s through 18.5 per cent in 1975 to 13.9 per cent in 1994. And yet surveys still regularly indicate that some 70 per cent of the population today believe in God. Diana herself was 'officially' a member of the Church of England – but it is clear that her spirituality was agglomerated from sources which lay well beyond the parameters of Anglicanism, Protestantism, Christianity, or even mainline religion. Hers was a 'DIY' faith – mixed and matched to her own personality, wants and desires. In this respect at least, it was characteristic of much contemporary First World spirituality – the kind of spirituality which gets increasingly described as 'postmodern'.

Postmodernity

In everyday language, we use the word 'modern' to define that which is 'up to date' and 'of the moment'. In a strictly chronological sense, what is modern is right here, right now, and to speak of things being 'post' the modern is nonsensical. But the word 'modern' can also be used in a more qualitative or thematic way. It often carries connotations of progress and development – of a confident march into the future.

Never was such confidence more robust than in the period which followed the Industrial Revolution of the eighteenth century. The years between 1730 and 1800 saw the invention of the fly-shuttle loom, the spinning jenny, the water-powered spinning frame and the steam engine; a national turnpike network was created in Britain, along with a countrywide system of canals. From these beginnings, there developed the heavy manufacturing industries of the nineteenth century and the mass production lines of the twentieth. In many ways, this technical advance represented the practical outworking of a growing emphasis on rationality and empirical deduction in the philosophy of the Enlightenment – that flowering of scientific and civic life which took root in the thought of Descartes, Spinoza and Liebnitz in the 1600s, and which blossomed into the great republican States inaugurated by the American and French Revolutions of the late eighteenth century.

Many people in the West still believe that the 'upward curve' of discovery which began in the Enlightenment will continue inexorably, and that as a result we shall all become better people. But as this last century has moved to its end, others have become more sceptical. They have realized that over the last one hundred years, factories turned out machine guns as well as fridge freezers; industrial processes led to Nazi death camps as well as to hospitals; and 'scientific progress' gave us chemical weapons as well as penicillin – the nuclear bomb as well as the incubator. High-rise tower blocks built on rationalistic principles to solve urban overcrowding have been vandalised, abandoned and blown up as unfit for human habitation. The centralized modern State, which began by proclaiming equality, liberty and fraternity, mutated into the tyranny of Stalin's Russia and the nightmare of Hitler's Germany. In the wake of all this, since the late '60s and early '70s, significant numbers of western academics and commentators have begun to question the supposition that to be 'modern' is in and of itself to be morally or spiritually superior to what has gone before – that technological progress alone can make us more 'whole' as people. This more sober, suspicious outlook is often nowadays described as 'postmodern', where the 'post' implies a 'hangover' from modernity – a 'comedown' from its more exalted claims and pretentions. While this comedown has included wide scale rejection of historic religious organizations – whose identity and function have often reflected those found in 'modern' industry and government – it has also offered new possibilities for religious faith and practice. From a Christian point of view, it could be said that in life, Diana explored these possibilities to both positive and negative effect. But it is even more important to realize that in death, she prompted many others to address such possibilities, and that the results of their doing so have been similarly double-edged.

In order to distinguish the pros and cons of the Princess' own search for transcendence, and of the spiritual reactions prompted by her death, it will be helpful to explore some key features of postmodernity, and to assess the significance of these features for the church post-Diana.

Key themes in postmodern spirituality and their relation to Diana's death

1. AMBIVALENCE

In 1991, the Polish philosopher Zygmunt Bauman in a seminal article defined the postmodern condition as 'living with ambivalence'. For Bauman, postmodern existence means 'existence devoid of certainty'. It is about living a 'contingent' life – a life free from eternal truths. It means abandoning faith in the order and design of the world. People living in ambivalence might show 'a preference for their own form of life', but they must never try to impose that form of life on others. As Bauman puts it – deliberately subverting Christian imagery – they must be 'immune to the temptation of cultural crusade'.

Bauman goes on to suggest that belief in ultimate or absolute truth leads inevitably to humiliation – humiliation of the other, the different, and the alien. Certainty is in this sense tantamount to imperialism and should be replaced by non-judgmental 'tolerance' and 'solidarity'. It is crucial to realize that ambivalence in this context does not mean simply indifference. It is taken in its more literal sense of 'upholding more than one state or possibility at the same time'. The late French cultural theorist Jean Francois Lyotard in 1979 summed up the postmodern condition as 'incredulity towards metanarratives'. By 'metanarrative' Lyotard meant any system of thought – any 'grand story' – which, like the Christian gospel, purports to legitimate and explain all other 'stories'. This was not to say that particular stories or explanations of the world had no currency; it just denied that any one of them could have absolute validity.

It is not difficult to see the implications of all this for spirituality in general – and Christian spirituality in particular. Religion began to get 'privatized' even before postmodernity, when the modern 'secular' state separated from the church and so pushed religion 'inward'. But at heart this was still one grand narrative gaining precedence over another: democracy usurping theocracy; the statute book usurping the Bible; economics usurping moral theology. In postmodernity, however, neither religion nor the state nor formal philosophy is allowed to mediate the 'big picture', since it is supposed that there are no big pictures to find, and that those who seek after them are guilty not only of self-deception, but of 'intolerance'.

Whatever we may think of ambivalence theologically, there can be little doubting its pervasiveness in contemporary western spirituality. Even if we emphasize the more positive definition of it as 'keeping options open', then, as I have suggested, Diana's own spirituality was thoroughly postmodern. But it was not only Diana who in these terms embodied postmodern spirituality. So, too, did the hundreds of thousands of people who thronged the streets of central London after her death, and the millions more who grieved in public places up and down the country.

If the postmodern situation is indeed characterized by ambivalence and 'uncertainty', then even in her death Diana highlighted the fact that on the spiritual level, Britain as a whole has become startlingly postmodern. When I got in a taxi on the Monday morning after Diana died, the female driver and I were not linked musically by the Biblical text of a classical Requiem, but by the tentative, all-purpose religiosity of Eric Clapton's 'Tears in Heaven', which the cabbie was playing repeatedly on her car stereo. When people needed to express their feelings symbolically, most eschewed clearly Christian emblems like the cross in favour of less 'marked' motifs: flowers, teddy bears and candles. Some estimated that there were 50 million individual blooms laid that week; plus 15,000 tons of assorted tributes, from cards to bottles of champagne, from poems to crockery bearing Diana's picture. This was deeply heartfelt, but hardly articulate or coherent. It was also a long way from being ecclesiastically 'orthodox'.

Then, of course, there was the memorial service at Westminster Abbey. It is typical of postmodern spirituality that the two elements of the service which had most impact on ordinary British people were Earl Spencer's tribute to his sister and Elton John and Bernie Taupin's specially rewritten version of 'Candle in the Wind'. The Earl's address was delivered from the pulpit and had many of the trappings of a sermon, but was hardly an exposition of the gospel. The Elton John song certainly deployed quasi-Christian imagery: it presented a redemptrix Diana as 'the grace that placed itself where lives were torn apart'; it envisioned Diana the Queen of Heaven, ascended to a place where 'the stars spell out [her] name'; and it nominated Diana as our country's 'lost soul' – its winged angel of compassion. If not actually idolatrous, this patchwork of sacred images was at least rather haphazard. These oddly displaced motifs summed up an event which seemed to hover all the time between the divine and the profane, the Christian and the sub-Christian, the official Anglican faith of the nation, and the folk religion of its people.

By recognizing and accommodating such ambivalence in the liturgy used, the Church of England did more than respond to popular sentiment; it powerfully formalized the shift from modern to postmodern spirituality in our culture.

2. PLURALISM

The postmodern world is more than simply ambivalent about absolute truth. It will often actively celebrate the differences of understanding and expression which result from that ambivalence. It both assumes and promotes pluralism – ie, the distinctions and diversities of culture, religion and belief.

For Isaiah Berlin, pluralism rests on the assumption that there is no final, fixed explanation of the world. It means a benign acceptance of the 'many different ends which [people] may seek'. Yet in an increasingly multicultural society, where these diverse strands of human life intersect, Berlin's liberality can easily develop into full-blown syncretism – that very 'pick and mix' approach to symbols, spiritualities and identities which Diana herself espoused, and which was so starkly displayed in the mass grieving which followed her death.

To a degree, of course, the spiritual pluralism of postmodern culture does foster the 'tolerance' and 'solidarity' which Zygmunt Bauman commends, and which Jesus himself modelled when he reached out to Gentile Centurions, Syro-Phoenecian women and Samaritans. Shortly after Diana died, the Principal of the Muslim College, Zaki Badawi, observed that the reaction of the Muslim community 'was identical to the rest of the population', and commended this as 'a sign of our growing integration'. He added that 'Diana's sensitivity to Islam, in adopting local dress on [a] visit to Pakistan, and the possibility that she might have been about to marry a Muslim, especially endeared her to us'.

But postmodern spiritual pluralism is not just about the mutuality of major world faiths. It is not so much distinguished by its concern to assimilate mainline religions as by its readiness to plunder them for what they can offer, and to rearrange their codes and practices into new patterns which bear scant relation to the original sources from which those codes and practices have derived. The social anthropologist Clifford Geertz offers a vivid illustration of this phenomenon:

A visitor to Japan wandered into a department store in Tokyo at the time when the Japanese had begun to take great interest in the symbolism of the Christmas season. And what symbol did the visitor discover prominently on display in the Tokyo department store? Santa Claus nailed to a cross!

This example belongs with the strangely incongruous, disjointed symbolism we saw along The Mall, and outside Kensington Palace, last September – with the portraits of the Virgin Mary held up beside the cuddly toys; the floral shrines surrounded by bottles of bubbly; the candles lit for vaguely apt pop ballads broadcast on portable radios. The pilgrim-as-consumer had, it seemed, come to pay homage to a new secular saint. The iconography of death had been cut loose from its moorings and left to float free from the old way of doing things. This brings us to a third dimension of postmodern spirituality.

3. ICONICITY

The Jewish academic George Steiner has written that the postmodern world seems to have nothing original left to say, and is typically content to reproduce, adapt, clone or send up what has gone before. Rather than always looking for novelty, postmodern culture self-consciously borrows and adapts from the past. It routinely proceeds on the assumption that there is 'nothing new under the sun'. Elton John's funeral rendition of 'Candle in the Wind' exemplified this, being an amended copy of one of his old hits from the 1970s.

In spiritual terms, Steiner goes on to recognize that rather than seeking fresh insight or revelation, pilgrims consciously look back into the past, borrowing from ancient wisdom and tailoring it to their current needs. As I write, the showbusiness world of California is turning excitedly to the Jewish Kabblalah – an esoteric branch of the faith which is actually practised by very few Jews today. Madonna, Roseanne Barr, Michael Jackson, Dave Stewart, George Harrison and several other stars have embraced it. As a sign of their devotion, they wear red wrist bands and necklaces, which represent Love, Spiritual

Enlightenment and friendship. But this is not Kabbalah as an Orthodox Rabbi would recognise it. It is Kabbalah as appropriated by the millionaire celebrity guru Deepak Chopra. Chopra was a student of the Maharishi Mahesh Yogi, who once famously taught the Beatles to meditate. His version of Kabbalah is Kabbalah off-the-peg; religion at an hourly fee.

Purists would say that this kind of postmodern spirituality is parasitic and plunders established belief-systems without respecting their integrity. The same sort of criticism has been levelled at the recent revival of Celtic Christianity. But in postmodernity, the original intentions which lie behind a set of symbols are less important than the symbols themselves. As the French postmodernist Jean Baudrillard has put it, 'the map precedes the territory'. Our simulacra – our analogical representations of the world – are no longer just 'secondary' to that world. If anything, they become anterior to it; they actually begin, in and of themselves, to constitute it. They take on a life of their own, so that image becomes reality and substance coalesces indissolubly with style.

Whatever the deeper philosophical validity of this position, it does bear out the willingness of much postmodern spirituality to let sacred symbols 'speak for themselves', without demanding that they refer in any fixed way to some definite or more literal truth. Just as the term 'iconicity' is used to describe the fusion of a signifier with the thing it is signifying, so we may say that much postmodern spirituality is 'iconic'. Whereas the icons of ancient Orthodoxy were 'windows' through which disciples could expect to perceive a divine 'other', postmodern iconicity is not so transparent. Its devotees typically stay with the symbol as such, rather than looking beyond it to a God 'on high'.

Such iconicity attached to Diana in life, but it has intensified remarkably since her death. Because she was the most photographed woman in the world, and because her development coincided with an unprecedented expansion in media and information technology, her image was all-pervasive and familiar. People could feel they knew her, even though most had never met her. In social, political and spiritual terms, Diana-as-icon became more significant than Diana Spencer of Althorp. Initially cast in the form of a fairytale princess, the icon later changed into a universal victim, and then into a herald of healing and peace. For all her brother's attempts to downplay such perceptions in his memorial address, the numinous images and extraordinary sales of 'Candle in the Wind' confirmed her postmodern elevation to divine status.

So, what exactly was being mourned in the days and weeks following that fatal car crash in Paris? This question prompts us to consider a further characteristic of postmodern spirituality.

4. INTROSPECTION

Just as postmodern spirituality is detached from organized religion, so it becomes increasingly 'self-service' in its ethos. Like Diana, we select from a range of devotional 'dishes' to suit our individual spiritual palette, rather than eating the 'set menu' provided by the church. Inevitably, religion becomes more introspective and less communal – more privatized and less corporate.

But where Diana's death is concerned, there is another aspect to this introspection. Over these last few months, I have choked back tears several times when I have come to reflect on her passing. Like so many others, I still cannot quite rationalize this, and am actually rather surprised by it. If I am honest, I was always rather exasperated by Diana. Then again, perhaps this is the point: as a postmodern icon, Diana may not offer a window into God; yet perhaps she does represent a mirror – a reflection not so much of our own spiritual aspirations, as of our own spiritual struggles and disappointments. Michael Ignatieff discerned this incisively: 'Our sorrow began with her and then eddied back upon ourselves. When we mourned her death, we mourned our own. People wept for their own mothers and fathers, for lost children, as if all the unconsoled losses of private life had been suddenly allowed to seek public consolation'.

5. PRAGMATIC COMPASSION

For all its self-regard, postmodern spirituality will at times paradoxically hanker for 'interconnectedness'. It does not expect religion to be uniform, but it hopes for some kind of harmony between the many different voices of conviction – some kind of global vision. This vision can be focused in ecological awareness and 'green' spiritualities such as those proposed by 'postmodern' theologians like Matthew Fox and Sallie MacFague. More often, however, it is expressed as a less clearly articulated desire for harmony between people. Another reason why Diana has so rapidly become an icon is that she is believed to have 'brought people together' as she took her 'gospel' of compassion to diverse tribes and nations – to AIDS victims and landmine casualties, to lepers and cancer patients, to Hindus, and Buddhists and Muslims. Indeed, marriage to the Muslim Dodi Fayed would have surely reinforced her status not only as the 'People's Princess', but also as a truly global 'Queen of Hearts', crossing the boundaries of creed, race and culture.

In her charity work, Diana exemplified the fact that postmodern spirituality is not simply contemplative, but also deeply pragmatic. It is committed to demonstrable care and concern. Married in the decade of Live Aid, Diana shared Bob Geldof's informal and 'unideological' approach to charity. This almost certainly flowed from the pragmatism of her own devotional life – from her readiness to change therapies and therapists according to what 'worked' for her, rather than according to any consistent worldview. The same kind of spiritual pragmatism was exhibited in the parks, squares and marketplaces of Britain during early September, as people customized established modes of grieving and constructed their own mourning-rituals 'on the hoof'.

Conclusion

The mass reaction to Diana's death has been viewed in some Christian quarters as a cause for optimism – a token of revival.

But we should be cautious. The church ought to be concerned that the confused, ad hoc, 'DIY' spirituality displayed in central London and elsewhere seemed for most people to have 'done the job' – to have assuaged their grief sufficiently, without recourse to organized religion.

It is true that the memorial service in Westminster Abbey managed deftly to weave the elements of postmodern spirituality we have been considering into a more traditional liturgical framework. At one level, it did the wider church a favour by putting the more aesthetically diverse, intimate, televisual, populist and globally-conscious strains of postmodern spirituality into the 'shop window' of public religion. But from a classical Christian perspective postmodern spirituality is at best a mixed blessing. Its ambivalence and pluralism means that while it is open and generous to different faith-communities, it is reluctant to commit itself finally to anything which might claim to be the faith. Its iconicity and introspection means that while it is willing to acknowledge and codify religious impulses, it is likely either to see those impulses as ends in themselves, or to turn them inward, rather than relating them to a God who is beyond us, as well as 'with us'. Its pragmatic compassion is often commendable, but, as Diana demonstrated, it will only go part way towards satisfying Douglas Coupland's quest for 'transcendence' and 'epiphany'. In this sense, her death did not so much leave a country 'lost without her soul', as expose a culture still oriented towards God, but increasingly unsure of how, or where, to find him.

BLOOD ON THEIR HANDS?

The role of the media

Heather Wraight

On December 3rd 1993 Diana, Princess of Wales, held a press conference at which she announced her intention to scale down her public duties. In her statement she said, 'When I started my public life 12 years ago, I understood that the media might be interested in what I did... But I was not aware of how overwhelming that attention would become; nor the extent to which it would affect both my public duties and my personal life...'

For many people, at least among the general public, the perception is that three and a half years later that 'overwhelming... attention' played a significant role in the Princess's death.

However, it was not only the general public who were sickened by what occurred in Paris on August 31st 1997. The week after Diana's funeral Libby Purves wrote in *The Times*, 'The trouble is that suddenly I don't want to be part of journalism any more.' In the months since the accident the focus of responsibility switched somewhat from the paparazzi to the influence of alcohol on the driver. Nevertheless there has never been any question that the Princess and her companion, Dodi Al Fayed, were being pursued by paparazzi that night, as they had been on previous occasions, especially during their recent holiday in the Mediterranean. It could be argued that if the lessons had been learned in 1993, the Princess might still be alive!

In the week leading up to the funeral many members of the public implied that all journalists should feel shame for what had happened. Part of that response is likely to be due to the commonly felt need to blame someone in order to try to cope with a sense of personal loss. However, why did Libby Purves and other journalists feel a sense of collective responsibility for the tragedy? Presumably because they felt their profession had been smeared, that they had 'blood on their hands' as the Princess's brother Earl Spencer so eloquently put it shortly after her death.

Journalism and professionalism

Journalism is considered one of the 'emerging professions', along with librarianship, social work, engineering, the police, architecture, accounting and other similar jobs. But what is a profession? Not only a way of making a living; it is the carrying out of an occupation to which standards of competence and responsibility are attached.

For the media those standards are laid down in professional Codes of Practice. The Dictionary goes on to describe the qualities that most people expect of a professional: a detailed knowledge, usually obtained by studying for a recognized qualification; a degree of competence in the practical skills involved; and the ability to use this skill and knowledge to provide a service for others. It follows that those on the receiving end of such services have the right to expect the standards to be met.

We tend to have the following expectations of the media, in particular of the reporting of news. These include: fairness, accuracy, relatively unbiased coverage (recognizing the bias to a particular political party of certain of the national daily newspapers), up-to-date, presentation of all opinions, not too parochial in scope, etc.

Various questions pose themselves, such as what constitutes news? Is Princess Diana having a holiday with Dodi Al Fayed actually news? And can the paparazzi be considered part of the media (and therefore may the same standards may be expected of them), or are they individuals responsible to no-one?

In the immediate aftermath of the Princess' tragic death, the key issue for the media was how the possibility of such a thing happening again could be reduced. Specifically, is it possible to control the paparazzi?

More important were the wider issues of reporting, such as what is and is not 'in the public interest'? On what sort of occasions is intrusion into personal privacy acceptable? How far can that intrusion go, even when it is justified?

Codes of practice

The most obvious outcome of these and other questions is that both the Press Complaints Commission and the Broadcasting Standards Commission have produced new Codes of Practice as a direct result of Diana's death. They define much more clearly matters such as accuracy, privacy, harassment, intrusion into grief or shock, and misrepresentation.

These Codes of Practice are generally agreed to be a significant improvement on the ones they replaced. However, the most obvious problem with them is that they remain voluntary. Despite several warnings by governments in recent years, the media in Britain continue to be allowed to practise self-regulation and there are no immediate plans to introduce a privacy law. While the media's Codes of Practice are worthy guidelines for day to day work, there is no way that they can be legally enforced. With no legal power to back them up, the responsibility for carrying them out rests on the shoulders of each individual practitioner.

One of the qualities expected of a professional is 'the personal integrity and discipline necessary to make a reasonable effort to meet the professional standards'.

The result is that this key issue for the media is still the same as it was in 1993 and in September 1997, albeit one step further on. The new Codes of Practice are a major improvement on the previous ones, but how can the industry ensure that they are followed? What issues create the kind of pressures which might drive journalists to break them?

Ethical dilemmas for the media

Ethical dilemmas arise in the media in several different ways. One means of identifying them is to examine them in relation to different aspects of communication. Communication theory has many models, but most of them in one way or another include the following segments: the message, the medium, the messenger and the receiver. The message is external to the media, it is the events in the surrounding world from which the media constitute news stories, which are reported in documentaries or on which they base dramas. The medium is the format itself: newspaper, radio – local or national, TV, video etc. Each of these functions in a slightly different way from the others. The messenger is the broadcaster or journalist whose task it is to put the message onto the medium. We will consider these three in turn:

1. THE EXTERNAL – These are dilemmas which arise because of the message which journalists want to convey and/or the public wish to read. These include:

   - When is news 'news' and not sensationalism or voyeurism?
   - What is the difference between something that is 'in the public interest' and something in which the public is interested?
   - Under what circumstances is it acceptable to buy material?
   - Where does the line come between a freelance photographer and a paparazzi?
   - How is the line drawn between facts, comment and conjecture?
   - To what extent can journalists eliminate personal bias and prejudice?

Most if not all of these pressures arose in the media coverage of Diana, Princess of Wales. For example, her campaign against landmines, or care for AIDS victims were clearly both newsworthy and in the public interest. But what about her personal relationships such as with Dodi Al Fayed? There is a distinct difference between something which is in the public interest and something in which the public is interested. During Diana's life, especially once her marriage to Prince Charles was known to be in trouble, there seemed to be an assumption both by the media and by the newspaper and magazine-buying public that people had the right to know as much as possible about the Princess, simply because they were interested in her.

It is clear that the Princess's relationship with the media was a 'love/hate' one. While she publicly blamed the media for creating pressure by their 'overwhelming... attention', she also used them especially as a kind of free advertizing for the issues about which she felt so passionately. Her campaign against landmines was cited as an example of an issue which is unlikely to have caught the public imagination in quite the same way if Princess Diana had not been photographed talking to landmine victims, or walking through a minefield.

For several years there has been in some quarters, especially among students, a boycott of Nestlé's products because of concern that babies in the Third World are being bottle-fed instead of breast-fed. Other similar boycotts occur from time to time. Yet no similar boycott has been exercised on the media as a result of their coverage of Princess Diana. When in November 1993 photos were published by the Daily Mirror of her working out in a gym, sales of the paper multiplied. There has never at any time been a suggestion that specific newspapers or broadcast programmes should be boycotted because of intrusive or offensive coverage of the Princess.

This is an area where there could be a Christian response. The Christian perspective is that each individual is of unique value to God, whether they be possibly the most photographed person who has ever lived or an ordinary citizen who is never likely to receive public acclaim. Christians, both as individuals and as wider bodies (be they churches or organizations) could play a role in challenging and encouraging the media to live up to their Codes of Practice. They could do this not only by drawing attention to failures or potential breaches of the Codes, but also by commending good practice (not only good programmes).

2. THE INTERNAL – the pressures created by the medium, which are an intrinsic part of the job, including:

- The constant tension between the freedom of the Press and the privacy of the individual that just because something is technically possible does not make it ethically acceptable. This is evident in the use of remote cameras or the electronic manipulation of photographs.
- The pressure of circulation figures and audience reach. Mary Kenny wrote, 'Diana's picture sells anything'.
- The 'snowball' effect – the broadsheet press did not buy photos of the Princess working out in a gymnasium in November 1993, but they did reproduce within their own condemnatory articles the photos which the Mirror had bought and published.
- The pressure to fill the air time or column inches within tight time constraints.
- That if Codes of Practice are too precise they are interpreted legalistically, if they are too vague they can easily be evaded.

Some media professionals recognize the validity of the list of potential pressures. But much wider issues are also at stake here, such as the breakdown of individual 'interior' ethics which has much to do with the erosion of willingness to accept authority. In modern society the 'bottom line' of success for the media is tied to circulation figures and audience ratings. Codes of Practice are based on underlying and rarely stated ethical values. They are also a form of authority. Unfortunately it is very easy for the pressure to succeed to drive journalists and others working in the media to push the Codes to the very limit without concern for the ethical values which arguably restrained a previous generation. Key things Christians can do in this respect are:

- To pray for those in the media.
- To seek to understand the issues they face, including ethical ones.
- To help Christians in the media to think through and wrestle with such issues.
- To encourage more Christians to go into the media and work towards positions of responsibility where they can influence the decision-making on such issues.

3. THE PERSONAL – how each individual 'messenger' makes judgements about ethical issues as they arise.

A person does not become a genuine professional when he accepts the standards for some reason other than his own belief in their excellence as professional standards... He must freely identify himself with the kind of person who admits and employs the proper standards of his profession.

Christians in, or interested in, the media need to be involved in discussion on personal responsibility in modern, or postmodern, society, the nature of society and the role of persons within it, and to think through the relevance of them to their own areas of work. Christians in the media need to be utterly professional, in the best sense of the word, setting a good example to those who might be tempted to cut corners ethically.

Conclusion

The new Codes of Practice are a significant step forward. However, these are voluntary and cannot be legally enforced, nor can the existence of a Code of Practice create moral behaviour. They are truly effective only when the people using them are motivated to fulfil them. Unless media practitioners act professionally by continually striving to maintain the ethical standards of the Codes of Practice, the sense of responsibility which was so evident in the months after the death of Diana Princess of Wales will gradually erode.